Functional Programming in C#:

: A Comprehensive Guide to Writing Elegant, Maintainable, and Efficient Code Using Functional Paradigms

Matthew D.Passmore

Table of content"

Chapter 6: Closures and Anonymous Functions

6.1 Understanding Closures in C#

6.2 Using Lambdas and Anonymous Functions Effectively

PART III: ADVANCED FUNCTIONAL PROGRAMMING TECHNIQUES

Chapter 7: Working with LINQ for Functional Programming

7.1 LINQ as a Functional Paradigm in C#

7.2 Advanced LINQ Queries and Transformations

Chapter 8: Pattern Matching and Deconstruction

8.1 Exploring Pattern Matching in C#

8.2 Using Deconstruction for Simplified Code

PART I: INTRODUCTION TO FUNCTIONAL PROGRAMMING IN C#

Chapter 1
Understanding Functional Programming

Functional programming is a programming paradigm that treats computation as the evaluation of mathematical functions and avoids changing state or mutable data. Unlike imperative programming, which focuses on describing how a program operates, functional programming emphasizes what should be computed.

Core Principles of Functional Programming:

Pure Functions: Functions that always produce the same output for the same input and have no side effects.
Immutability: Data cannot be modified once created, ensuring a predictable state.
First-Class Functions: Functions are treated as values, meaning they can be assigned to variables, passed as arguments, and returned from other functions.

Function Composition: Combining small, reusable functions to create more complex behaviors.

Benefits of Functional Programming:

Maintainability: Code is easier to understand and debug due to predictable behavior.
Reusability: Pure functions and immutability promote modular, reusable components.
Concurrency: Immutability eliminates issues with shared state in multi-threaded environments.

Scalability: Functional code is well-suited for modern applications requiring high performance and reliability.

In C#, functional programming features such as LINQ, lambdas, and immutability provide powerful tools for adopting this paradigm, enabling developers to write clean, efficient, and maintainable code.

1.1 What is Functional Programming?

Functional programming is a programming paradigm that focuses on building software by composing pure functions and avoiding shared state, mutable data, and side effects. It emphasizes a declarative style, describing what to do rather than how to do it, making code more predictable and easier to debug.

Key Characteristics of Functional Programming:

Pure Functions: Functions that produce the same output for the same input and have no side effects (e.g., modifying global variables or interacting with I/O).

Immutability: Data is immutable, meaning it cannot be changed after it is created. Instead, new data structures are created when modifications are needed.

First-Class Functions: Functions are treated as first-class citizens, meaning they can be assigned to variables, passed as arguments, and returned from other functions.

Higher-Order Functions: Functions that take other functions as arguments or return them as results.

Function Composition: Combining smaller, reusable functions to build more complex operations.

Benefits of Functional Programming:

Modularity and Reusability: Pure functions and immutability make code easier to test, debug, and reuse.

Easier Parallelism: Since there is no shared mutable state, functional programs are naturally thread-safe and suitable for concurrent programming.

Declarative Style: Code describes what to compute, reducing complexity and improving readability.

Functional Programming in C#

C# supports functional programming concepts such as lambda expressions, LINQ, pattern matching, and immutable data structures, enabling developers to write more elegant, maintainable, and efficient code by leveraging functional paradigms alongside its object-oriented features.

1.2 Benefits of Functional Programming in Modern Software Development

Functional programming (FP) is increasingly popular in modern software development due to its ability to produce clean, maintainable, and scalable code. Here are some of its key benefits:

1. Improved Code Maintainability

Pure functions and immutability ensure that functions are predictable and have no hidden side effects, making it easier to debug and maintain code over time.
The declarative style allows developers to focus on what needs to be done rather than how, resulting in more readable code.

2. Enhanced Modularity and Reusability

FP encourages writing small, reusable functions that are easier to test and combine.
Higher-order functions and function composition provide powerful tools for reusing logic across applications.

3. Better Concurrency and Parallelism

Immutability and the absence of shared mutable state eliminate common concurrency issues like race conditions.
Functional programs are naturally thread-safe, making them ideal for parallel processing and distributed systems.

4. Reduced Bugs and Easier Testing

Pure functions are deterministic, meaning they always produce the same output for the same input, simplifying unit testing.

Immutable data structures prevent accidental state changes, reducing the likelihood of subtle bugs.

5. Scalability for Modern Applications

Functional programming is well-suited for large-scale applications where scalability, reliability, and performance are critical.

Frameworks and tools leveraging functional paradigms, such as Reactive Extensions (Rx), make it easier to manage complex, event-driven systems.

6. Declarative Code for Enhanced Productivity

Developers can write less boilerplate code and express complex logic more concisely with constructs like LINQ in C#.

FP facilitates a higher level of abstraction, reducing cognitive load and enabling faster development cycles.

7. Seamless Integration with Other Paradigms

In languages like C#, FP integrates well with object-oriented programming (OOP), allowing developers to leverage the strengths of both paradigms.

This hybrid approach makes it easier to adopt FP incrementally without overhauling existing codebases.

By incorporating functional programming techniques, modern software development becomes more robust, efficient, and adaptable to the demands of complex systems and applications.

1.3 Imperative vs. Functional Paradigms

The imperative and functional paradigms are two distinct approaches to programming, each with its own principles, strengths, and use cases. Understanding their differences can help developers choose the right paradigm for their application needs.

Imperative Programming Paradigm

Imperative programming focuses on explicitly describing how a program operates. It uses step-by-step instructions to manipulate program state and achieve the desired result.

Key Features:

State and Mutability: Relies on changing variables and maintaining program state throughout execution.
Control Flow: Utilizes loops (for, while) and conditional statements (if-else) to control program behavior.
Procedural Logic: Code is often organized into procedures or methods that execute instructions sequentially.

Advantages:

Easy to learn and widely used in beginner programming courses.
Direct mapping to hardware instructions makes it efficient for low-level operations.
Familiar structure for developers with experience in procedural or object-oriented programming.

Disadvantages:

Managing state and mutability can lead to bugs, especially in complex systems.
Difficult to scale for parallel or concurrent tasks.
Code tends to be less modular and harder to maintain.

Functional Programming Paradigm

Functional programming focuses on what to compute rather than how to compute it. It uses mathematical functions to describe relationships and transformations, avoiding mutable state and side effects.

Key Features:

Immutability: Data is immutable, and any changes result in new data structures.
Pure Functions: Functions are independent of program state and external data, always producing the same output for the same input.
Declarative Style: Developers describe the logic of computation without focusing on control flow or state changes.

Advantages:

Easier to test and debug due to the predictability of pure functions.

Naturally supports parallelism and concurrency because there is no shared mutable state.

Modular and reusable code through higher-order functions and function composition.

Disadvantages:

Steeper learning curve for developers unfamiliar with the paradigm.

Potential for reduced performance if immutability is not optimized.

Not always intuitive for certain tasks, like low-level hardware operations.

Comparison: Imperative vs. Functional

Aspect	Imperative Paradigm	Functional Paradigm
Focus	How to perform tasks	What to compute

State Management	Mutable, often global	Immutable, localized
Control Flow	Explicit (loops, conditionals)	Implicit (recursion, higher-order functions)
Modularity	Procedures and methods	Pure functions and composition
Concurrency	Challenging due to shared state	Easier with immutability
Code Style	Procedural, step-by-step	Declarative, concise

,

When to Use Each Paradigm

Imperative Programming:

Best for scenarios requiring detailed control of hardware, system-level programming, or situations where performance and direct memory manipulation are critical (e.g., embedded systems).

Functional Programming:

Ideal for applications requiring high scalability, parallelism, or complex business logic (e.g., web services, data pipelines).

By understanding both paradigms, developers can leverage their strengths to build efficient and maintainable software solutions. Many modern languages, like C#, support both paradigms, allowing developers to choose the best approach for their use case.

Chapter 2
C# as a Functional Language

While traditionally known as an object-oriented language, C# has evolved to support functional programming features, making it a hybrid language that allows developers to incorporate functional paradigms alongside its object-oriented capabilities.

Key Functional Features in C#:

Lambda Expressions: Compact syntax for defining anonymous functions, commonly used in LINQ and higher-order functions.

LINQ (Language-Integrated Query): A declarative approach to data processing, enabling concise and readable operations on collections.

Immutable Data Structures: Libraries like System.Collections.Immutable provide data structures that ensure immutability.

Pattern Matching: Introduced in recent versions, pattern matching simplifies working with complex data structures in a functional style.

Higher-Order Functions: Methods like Select, Where, and Aggregate allow passing functions as arguments for transformation and filtering operations.

Tuples and Deconstruction: Enables returning multiple values and breaking them into smaller parts for cleaner, more functional code.

Records: Immutable data types introduced in C# 9, ideal for modeling data in a functional style.

Benefits of Functional Programming in C#:

Improves code readability and maintainability with declarative constructs.

Reduces bugs by promoting immutability and pure functions.

Simplifies concurrency and parallelism through thread-safe, immutable designs.

C# strikes a balance between functional and object-oriented paradigms, enabling developers to adopt functional programming incrementally without sacrificing the benefits of its traditional features.

2.1 Overview of Functional Features in C#

C# is a versatile language that has embraced functional programming principles, allowing developers to write cleaner, more modular, and maintainable code. These functional features complement its object-oriented roots, making C# a powerful choice for modern application development.

1. Lambda Expressions

Lambda expressions provide a concise way to define anonymous functions. They are heavily used in LINQ and other scenarios requiring functions as arguments.

Example:

```csharp
Copy code
var squares = numbers.Select(x => x * x);
```

Lambda expressions simplify code, especially when working with higher-order functions.

2. LINQ (Language-Integrated Query)

LINQ enables declarative querying of data sources such as collections, databases, or XML. It promotes a functional style by abstracting loops and conditions into concise expressions.

Example:

csharp
Copy code
```csharp
var evenNumbers = numbers.Where(n => n % 2 == 0).ToList();
```

3. Immutable Data Structures

The System.Collections.Immutable namespace provides collections like ImmutableList, ImmutableDictionary, and more, ensuring data immutability. This reduces unintended side effects and simplifies concurrency.
Example:

csharp
Copy code

```csharp
var immutableList = ImmutableList.Create(1, 2, 3);
```

4. Higher-Order Functions

C# supports functions that take other functions as arguments or return them as results. Common examples include LINQ methods like Select, Where, and Aggregate.

Example:

csharp
Copy code
```csharp
var sum = numbers.Aggregate(0, (total, next) => total + next);
```

5. Pattern Matching
Introduced in C# 7 and enhanced in later versions, pattern matching enables concise and expressive handling of data structures and logic.

Example:

csharp

```
Copy code
string message = age switch
{
    < 18 => "Minor",
    >= 18 and < 60 => "Adult",
    _ => "Senior"
};
```

6. Tuples and Deconstruction

C# allows returning multiple values using tuples and breaking them down into individual components, aligning with functional programming's emphasis on simplicity. Example:

csharp
Copy code
```
(string name, int age) person = ("Alice", 30);
var (name, age) = person;
```

7. Records

Records, introduced in C# 9, are immutable reference types designed for data modeling. They promote immutability and functional-style data handling.
Example:

csharp
Copy code
```csharp
public record Person(string Name, int Age);
```

8. Expression-Bodied Members

Expression-bodied members simplify method, property, or constructor definitions, encouraging a functional style.
Example:

csharp
Copy code
```csharp
public int Square(int x) => x * x;
```

9. Local Functions
C# allows defining functions inside methods, improving code organization and readability.

Example:

```csharp
Copy code
void ProcessNumbers()
{
    int Square(int x) => x * x;
    Console.WriteLine(Square(5));
}
```

10. Async and Task-Based Programming

While not strictly functional, C#'s asynchronous programming model aligns well with functional principles, especially when paired with immutability and pure functions.

Conclusion

C# provides robust functional programming features that enable developers to write elegant, maintainable, and scalable applications. By blending functional and object-oriented paradigms, C# empowers developers to choose the best approach for their specific needs, making it a modern and versatile language.

2.2 The Evolution of Functional Programming in C#

C# began as a predominantly object-oriented programming (OOP) language but has progressively embraced functional programming (FP) concepts over its many iterations. This evolution has been driven by the need for developers to write more modular, concise, and maintainable code, as well as to address challenges such as concurrency and scalability in modern software development.

C# 1.0 (2002): The Foundations

The earliest versions of C# were firmly rooted in object-oriented principles, with no direct support for functional programming.
Delegates were introduced as a foundation for functional programming, allowing methods to be passed as arguments.

Example of a delegate in C# 1.0:

csharp
Copy code

```csharp
public delegate int Operation(int x, int y);
```

C# 2.0 (2005): Opening the Door to FP

Anonymous Methods: Allowed inline definition of delegates without requiring separate named methods, simplifying code.
Generics: Provided the groundwork for reusable and type-safe higher-order functions, enhancing functional programming capabilities.

Example of an anonymous method:

csharp
Copy code
```csharp
Action<int> print = delegate (int x) { Console.WriteLine(x); };
```

C# 3.0 (2007): The FP Revolution

Lambda Expressions: Introduced a concise syntax for creating anonymous functions, which became a cornerstone of functional programming in C#.

LINQ (Language-Integrated Query): Enabled declarative data manipulation, a hallmark of functional programming.
Expression Trees: Allowed treating code as data, enabling advanced functional programming techniques like building dynamic queries.

Example of LINQ with lambda expressions:

csharp
Copy code
```
var evenNumbers = numbers.Where(x => x % 2 == 0);
```

C# 4.0 (2010): Consolidation

Functional programming features were further refined, though no major new FP features were introduced.
Enhanced support for dynamic types indirectly benefited functional programming by improving flexibility.

C# 5.0 (2012): Concurrency and Async

Async/Await: Revolutionized asynchronous programming, which aligns with functional principles like immutability and composability.

Example of async/await:

csharp
Copy code
```csharp
public async Task<int> GetDataAsync() => await Task.Run(() => 42);
```

C# 6.0 (2015): Conciseness and Readability

Expression-Bodied Members: Simplified methods and properties into single-line expressions.
Enhanced lambda expression syntax and null-conditional operators (?.) promoted a functional style.

C# 7.0 and Beyond (2017–Present): Modern

Functional Features
Pattern Matching: Provided a functional way to handle complex branching logic.
Tuples and Deconstruction: Simplified returning and working with multiple values, improving functional workflows.
Local Functions: Enabled defining functions within other functions, enhancing modularity.

Immutable Data Structures: While not part of the core language, libraries like System.Collections.Immutable became increasingly popular.

C# 9.0 (2020): Immutability with Records

Records: A major leap toward functional programming, allowing concise, immutable data modeling.

Example of a record:

```csharp
Copy code
public record Person(string Name, int Age);
```

C# Today: A Hybrid Approach

Modern C# is a hybrid language, blending the best of functional and object-oriented programming paradigms. Developers can write purely functional modules using LINQ, immutable types, and higher-order functions, while still leveraging OOP where needed.

Conclusion

The evolution of functional programming in C# reflects the language's adaptability and responsiveness to modern software development challenges. By integrating functional features incrementally, C# enables developers to adopt functional programming practices alongside its rich object-oriented ecosystem, offering the best of both worlds.

2.3 Why Choose C# for Functional Programming?

C# has become a compelling choice for functional programming due to its versatile nature, blending the best aspects of object-oriented programming (OOP) and functional programming (FP). With its extensive toolset, modern syntax, and continuous evolution, C# offers developers the ability to write cleaner, more maintainable, and scalable code using functional paradigms.

1. Versatility as a Multi-Paradigm Language

C# seamlessly integrates functional programming features with its object-oriented core, allowing developers to choose the best paradigm for the task at hand. This flexibility makes C# ideal for teams and projects that benefit from a combination of approaches.

2. Strong Support for Functional Concepts

C# includes many features that align with functional programming principles, such as:

Immutability: Support for immutable data structures via records and the System.Collections.Immutable namespace.
Higher-Order Functions: Methods like Select, Where, and Aggregate allow passing and returning functions as arguments.

Pure Functions: Developers can leverage pure functions to improve code predictability and reliability.
Declarative Syntax: LINQ provides a functional and expressive way to query and manipulate data.

Example using LINQ:

csharp

Copy code

```
var evenNumbers = numbers.Where(n => n % 2 == 0).ToList();
```

3. Modern and Evolving Language

With every version, C# incorporates new functional programming features, such as:

Pattern Matching: Simplifies branching logic with declarative syntax.
Records: Introduced in C# 9, enabling concise and immutable data modeling.
Local Functions and Tuples: Allow better modularity and data manipulation.

4. Readable and Maintainable Code

Functional programming in C# promotes clean, concise, and declarative code, making it easier to understand and maintain. Immutability and pure functions reduce side effects, resulting in fewer bugs and better testability.

5. Simplified Concurrency and Parallelism

Functional programming principles like immutability and stateless functions align perfectly with concurrent and parallel programming. Features like asynchronous programming with async/await and thread-safe collections make it easier to write scalable and high-performance applications.

Example of concurrency:

csharp
Copy code
```
var tasks = data.Select(async item => await ProcessAsync(item));
await Task.WhenAll(tasks);
```

6. Seamless Integration with the .NET Ecosystem

The .NET platform provides robust tools, libraries, and frameworks that support functional programming in C#. Developers can take advantage of powerful tools like LINQ, Entity Framework, and libraries for immutable collections without needing external dependencies.

7. Incremental Adoption

C# allows developers to gradually adopt functional programming. Teams familiar with OOP can begin incorporating FP features like LINQ, lambda expressions, and immutability without completely overhauling their approach.

Use Cases for C# in Functional Programming

C#'s functional capabilities make it suitable for a variety of scenarios, including:

Data Transformation and Querying: Leveraging LINQ for concise and powerful data manipulation.
Event-Driven Applications: Pure functions and immutability simplify state management.
Concurrent Systems: Stateless and thread-safe functional programming reduces concurrency issues.

Conclusion

C# is an excellent choice for functional programming, offering a rich set of features that align with FP principles while maintaining its roots in OOP. Its flexibility, modern syntax, and robust ecosystem make it ideal for developers looking to write elegant, maintainable, and high-performance code in a functional style.

PART II: CORE CONCEPTS OF FUNCTIONAL PROGRAMMING

Chapter 3
First-Class and Higher-Order Functions

First-class functions treat functions as regular values, meaning they can be assigned to variables, passed as arguments, or returned as results. This capability allows developers to write flexible and reusable code.

Example of a first-class function in C#:

```csharp
Copy code
Func<int, int, int> add = (x, y) => x + y;
Console.WriteLine(add(3, 5)); // Output: 8
```

Higher-order functions are functions that either take other functions as arguments or return functions as results. These are foundational in functional programming and enable abstraction over actions.

Example of a higher-order function in C#:

csharp

Copy code

```csharp
static int PerformOperation(int a, int b, Func<int, int,
int> operation)
{
    return operation(a, b);
}

// Usage
Console.WriteLine(PerformOperation(10, 20, (x, y) =>
x + y)); // Output: 30
```

C#'s support for lambda expressions, delegates, and LINQ
makes it easy to implement first-class and higher-order
functions, enhancing code modularity and reusability.

3.1 Defining and Using First-Class Functions

First-class functions are a key concept in functional
programming, where functions are treated as first-class
citizens. In C#, this means that functions can be assigned to

variables, passed as arguments, and returned from other functions, just like any other object or data type. This flexibility allows for more expressive and reusable code, especially in the context of functional programming paradigms.

Defining First-Class Functions in C#

In C#, first-class functions are typically defined using delegates, Func, and Action types, or through lambda expressions. These constructs allow functions to be treated as values that can be assigned, passed around, or returned.

Using Lambda Expressions

Lambda expressions are a concise way to define anonymous functions, which can be assigned to variables or passed as arguments.

Example:

csharp
Copy code
```csharp
Func<int, int, int> add = (x, y) => x + y;
Console.WriteLine(add(3, 4)); // Output: 7
```

Using Delegates

Delegates are type-safe function pointers that can reference methods and allow functions to be passed as arguments.

Example:

csharp
Copy code
```csharp
public delegate int MathOperation(int x, int y);

MathOperation add = (x, y) => x + y;
Console.WriteLine(add(5, 3)); // Output: 8
```

Using Func and Action Types

The Func type is used for functions that return a value, while Action is used for functions that return void. Both types can represent first-class functions in C#.

Example with Func:

csharp
Copy code

```csharp
Func<int, int, int> multiply = (x, y) => x * y;
Console.WriteLine(multiply(4, 6)); // Output: 24
```

Using First-Class Functions

Once a function is defined as a first-class citizen, it can be used in various ways to create more modular and flexible code.

Passing Functions as Arguments

Functions can be passed as arguments to other functions, enabling high-order abstractions. This is commonly used in methods like LINQ or custom higher-order functions.

Example:

```csharp
Copy code
static int ApplyOperation(int x, int y, Func<int, int, int> operation)
{
    return operation(x, y);
}
```

Console.WriteLine(ApplyOperation(3, 4, (x, y) => x * y)); // Output: 12

Returning Functions from Other Functions

Functions can also be returned from other functions, allowing dynamic function creation based on input parameters.

Example:

csharp
Copy code
```csharp
static Func<int, int> MultiplyBy(int factor)
{
    return (x) => x * factor;
}
```

var multiplyByTwo = MultiplyBy(2);
Console.WriteLine(multiplyByTwo(5)); // Output: 10

Storing Functions in Collections

Functions can be stored in collections (e.g., arrays, lists), making it easy to apply a set of functions in a loop or dynamically invoke them.

Example:

csharp
Copy code

```csharp
List<Func<int, int>> operations = new List<Func<int, int>>()
{
    (x) => x + 1,
    (x) => x * 2,
    (x) => x - 3
};

foreach (var operation in operations)
{
    Console.WriteLine(operation(5));  // Output: 6, 10, 2
}
```

Benefits of First-Class Functions

Modularity: First-class functions promote cleaner and more modular code by enabling small, reusable functions that can be composed together.

Flexibility: Functions can be dynamically chosen or created based on runtime conditions, making code more flexible and adaptable.

Abstraction: First-class functions allow you to abstract common behaviors into reusable components, reducing redundancy.

Declarative Programming: When functions are passed as arguments or returned from other functions, it encourages a declarative style of programming that can make code more readable and maintainable.

Conclusion

In C#, first-class functions enable developers to write more flexible, modular, and reusable code. By leveraging lambda expressions, delegates, and Func/Action types, functions can be treated as values that can be assigned, passed, and returned just like any other data type. This capability unlocks powerful functional programming patterns and facilitates cleaner and more maintainable software development.

3.2 Higher-Order Functions Explained with Examples

Higher-order functions (HOFs) are a powerful concept in functional programming. A higher-order function is a function that either:

Takes one or more functions as arguments.
Returns a function as its result.
This concept is a key feature of functional programming, enabling more abstract, reusable, and flexible code. In C#, higher-order functions can be easily implemented using lambda expressions, delegates, and Func types.

Higher-Order Functions in C#

C# fully supports higher-order functions. By passing and returning functions, you can create more modular and declarative code. Here's a breakdown of how HOFs work and how you can define and use them in C#.

1. Passing Functions as Arguments

A higher-order function can take another function as an argument, enabling dynamic behavior based on the provided function. This approach allows greater flexibility in how operations are applied.

Example:

```csharp
Copy code
// Higher-order function that accepts a function as a parameter
static int ApplyOperation(int a, int b, Func<int, int, int> operation)
{
    return operation(a, b);
}

var add = (x, y) => x + y;
var multiply = (x, y) => x * y;

Console.WriteLine(ApplyOperation(5, 3, add)); // Output: 8
Console.WriteLine(ApplyOperation(5, 3, multiply)); // Output: 15
```

In this example, ApplyOperation is a higher-order function that takes a function (operation) as an argument. The add and multiply functions are passed to ApplyOperation, demonstrating the flexibility of higher-order functions.

2. Returning Functions from Other Functions

Higher-order functions can also return functions. This allows the creation of more specialized functions based on input parameters or external conditions.

Example:

```csharp
Copy code
// Higher-order function that returns another function
static Func<int, int> MultiplyBy(int factor)
{
    return x => x * factor;
}

var multiplyByTwo = MultiplyBy(2);
var multiplyByThree = MultiplyBy(3);
```

Console.WriteLine(multiplyByTwo(5)); // Output: 10
Console.WriteLine(multiplyByThree(5)); // Output: 15

In this case, MultiplyBy is a higher-order function that takes a factor and returns a new function that multiplies its input by the specified factor. The returned function is then invoked with specific arguments.

3. Combining Functions with Higher-Order Functions

Higher-order functions can also combine multiple functions into one. This allows you to compose and chain operations, creating a more declarative style of programming.

Example:

csharp
Copy code
```
// Higher-order function that combines two functions
into one
static Func<int, int> Compose(Func<int, int> f,
Func<int, int> g)
{
```

```
    return x => f(g(x));
}

var addOne = (x) => x + 1;
var multiplyByTwo = (x) => x * 2;

var addThenMultiply = Compose(addOne, multiplyByTwo);
Console.WriteLine(addThenMultiply(3)); // Output: 7
(3 * 2 + 1)
```

In this example, Compose is a higher-order function that takes two functions (f and g) and returns a new function that applies g first and then f. The composition allows chaining operations together.

4. Using Higher-Order Functions with LINQ

LINQ (Language Integrated Query) is an excellent example of how higher-order functions are used in C#. Many LINQ methods (like Select, Where, and Aggregate) are higher-order functions that accept delegates or lambda expressions as arguments.

Example with Select:

csharp

Copy code

```csharp
var numbers = new[] { 1, 2, 3, 4, 5 };

// Higher-order function: Select takes a function as an argument
var squaredNumbers = numbers.Select(x => x * x);

Console.WriteLine(string.Join(", ", squaredNumbers));
// Output: 1, 4, 9, 16, 25
```

In this case, Select is a higher-order function that takes a lambda function (x => x * x) as an argument and applies it to each element in the array, returning a new collection.

Benefits of Higher-Order Functions

Code Reusability: HOFs allow you to write more generic and reusable code, as you can pass any function as an argument or return different functions based on input.

Declarative Programming: Higher-order functions promote a more declarative style, where the focus is on what needs to be done, not how it's done.

Composability: They make it easy to compose complex behaviors by combining simple functions into new functions, leading to cleaner, more readable code.

Abstraction: HOFs help abstract common patterns of computation, reducing redundancy and making the code easier to maintain.

Conclusion

Higher-order functions are a powerful feature of functional programming, and C# provides robust support for them. By allowing functions to be passed as arguments or returned as results, higher-order functions enable developers to write more modular, reusable, and expressive code. This flexibility leads to cleaner, more declarative, and maintainable code that is easier to reason about and extend.

Chapter 4

Immutability in C#: The Cornerstone of Functional Programming

Immutability is a core concept in functional programming, emphasizing that data should not be modified after it is created. In C#, immutability ensures that once an object or variable is assigned a value, it cannot be changed, which leads to safer, more predictable code.

Why Immutability Matters

Thread Safety: Immutable objects can be shared safely across multiple threads without the need for synchronization.

Predictability: With immutability, functions and operations become more predictable because their outputs are solely determined by their inputs.

Simplified Debugging: Since immutable objects cannot change state, it reduces the complexity of tracking down bugs related to data mutations.

Implementing Immutability in C#

In C#, immutability is typically achieved by using readonly fields, const variables, or by defining properties with only getters and no setters.

Example of Immutability with a Class:

```csharp
Copy code
public class Person
{
    public string Name { get; }
    public int Age { get; }

    public Person(string name, int age)
    {
        Name = name;
        Age = age;
```

```
    }
}
```

var person = new Person("Alice", 30);
// person.Age = 31; // Error: cannot modify the property

In this example, the Person class is immutable because the properties Name and Age can only be set through the constructor and cannot be modified after creation.

Benefits of Immutability

No Side Effects: Functions that deal with immutable data avoid unexpected changes to data, ensuring side-effect-free operations.
Ease of Concurrency: Since data cannot change, there's no need for locks or other concurrency controls, making it easier to build multithreaded applications.
Cleaner Code: Immutability encourages functional patterns like map, filter, and reduce, leading to concise, declarative code.

In C#, while mutability is common, embracing immutability in the right places helps unlock many of the benefits of functional programming, particularly in building robust, concurrent, and maintainable applications.

4.1 What is Immutability?

Immutability is a concept in programming where an object's state cannot be modified after it is created. Once an immutable object is initialized with a value, that value remains constant throughout its lifecycle, ensuring no changes can be made to its internal state.

In contrast to mutable objects, which allow modification of their state after creation, immutable objects protect data from being altered, which helps to avoid issues like unintended side effects, race conditions, or inconsistent state changes.

Key Characteristics of Immutability:

No State Modification: Once an immutable object is initialized, its properties cannot be changed.
Safer Code: Immutability makes code more predictable and safer, especially in concurrent environments, because

multiple threads can safely access immutable data without the risk of it being modified.

Simplified Debugging: Immutable objects ensure that their state remains consistent, which can reduce the complexity of tracking down bugs related to unexpected changes in data.

Example of Immutability in C#:

In C#, you can implement immutability by using properties with only getters (no setters), or by marking fields as readonly to prevent changes after initialization.

Example with an Immutable Class:

```csharp
Copy code
public class Person
{
    public string Name { get; }
    public int Age { get; }

    public Person(string name, int age)
    {
        Name = name;
        Age = age;
```

```
    }
}
```

// Creating an immutable object
var person = new Person("Alice", 30);

// person.Name = "Bob"; // Error: cannot modify the
property
In this example, the Person class is immutable because the properties Name and Age can only be set through the constructor and cannot be changed afterward.

Benefits of Immutability:

Thread Safety: Multiple threads can safely access the same immutable object without the need for synchronization, as there is no risk of data modification.
Predictability: Functions operating on immutable objects are more predictable, as their behavior is based purely on their input, without hidden side effects.
Easier Debugging: With no unexpected changes to data, debugging becomes simpler and more reliable.

Immutability is a fundamental principle of functional programming, as it helps to maintain the integrity and consistency of data throughout the application's execution.

4.2 Implementing Immutability in C# Applications

Immutability is a core principle of functional programming, and it can significantly enhance the reliability, maintainability, and readability of your C# applications. Implementing immutability ensures that once an object or variable is created, its state cannot be modified, helping to reduce unintended side effects, improve thread safety, and make code easier to reason about.

Here's how you can implement immutability in C#:

1. Using readonly Fields

In C#, the readonly keyword ensures that a field can only be assigned a value once, either at the point of declaration or in the constructor. Once assigned, the value cannot be changed.

Example:

```csharp
Copy code
public class Person
{
    public readonly string Name;
    public readonly int Age;

    public Person(string name, int age)
    {
        Name = name;
        Age = age;
    }
}
```

In this example, both Name and Age are readonly, meaning their values can only be set during object initialization and cannot be modified afterward.

2. Using Immutable Collections

C# provides a range of immutable collection classes in the System.Collections.Immutable namespace, including

ImmutableList,   ImmutableDictionary,   and
ImmutableArray. These collections ensure that once they are
created, their elements cannot be changed.

Example:

```csharp
Copy code
using System.Collections.Immutable;

public class ShoppingCart
{
    public ImmutableList<string> Items { get; }

    public ShoppingCart()
    {
        Items = ImmutableList<string>.Empty;
    }

    public ShoppingCart AddItem(string item)
    {
        return new ShoppingCart { Items = Items.Add(item) };
    }
}
```

```csharp
var cart = new ShoppingCart();
var updatedCart = cart.AddItem("Apple");
```

In this example, the Items collection is immutable. Whenever a new item is added, it creates and returns a new ShoppingCart object, rather than modifying the original.

3. Read-Only Properties

Another approach to implementing immutability is by defining properties with only getters and no setters. This ensures that the property values cannot be modified after the object is created.

Example:

csharp
Copy code
```csharp
public class Product
{
    public string Name { get; }
    public decimal Price { get; }

    public Product(string name, decimal price)
```

```csharp
{
    Name = name;
    Price = price;
}
}
```

Here, the Product class is immutable because the properties Name and Price can only be set during object initialization and cannot be changed afterward.

4. Using Tuples and Records (C# 9 and Later)

C# 9 introduced records, a new feature designed specifically for immutable data structures. Records provide a succinct syntax for defining immutable objects, along with built-in support for value-based equality comparisons.

Example:

```csharp
csharp
Copy code
public record Book(string Title, string Author, decimal Price);

// Creating an immutable object
```

```csharp
var book = new Book("C# Programming", "John Doe", 29.99m);

// book.Title = "New Title"; // Error: cannot modify the property
```

In this example, the Book record is immutable, and its properties are initialized via the constructor. The value of the object cannot be changed after it has been created.

5. Avoiding Setter Methods

To enforce immutability, avoid defining setter methods for fields or properties. This prevents any modification of the object's state after it is created. You can use constructor injection to set values and make properties read-only.

Example:

```csharp
csharp
Copy code
public class Customer
{
    public string Name { get; }
    public int Age { get; }
```

```csharp
public Customer(string name, int age)
{
    Name = name;
    Age = age;
}
}
```

In this example, Customer class properties are read-only, ensuring that once a Customer object is created, its values cannot be modified.

6. Using Functional Programming Patterns

Functional programming patterns, such as pure functions and immutable transformations, can be used to enforce immutability throughout your C# application. For instance, instead of modifying an object, return a new instance with the desired state.

Example:

```csharp
Copy code
public class Order
```

```
{
    public string Item { get; }
    public int Quantity { get; }

    public Order(string item, int quantity)
    {
        Item = item;
        Quantity = quantity;
    }

    public Order WithNewQuantity(int newQuantity)
    {
        return new Order(Item, newQuantity); // Returns
a new Order object
    }
}
```

The WithNewQuantity method does not alter the original
Order object but instead returns a new Order with the
updated quantity.

7. Immutable Structs

You can also define immutable structs in C#. To do so, make sure that all fields in the struct are readonly and that there are no setters for properties.

Example:

```csharp
Copy code
public readonly struct Point
{
    public int X { get; }
    public int Y { get; }

    public Point(int x, int y)
    {
        X = x;
        Y = y;
    }
}
```

The Point struct is immutable because the X and Y properties are readonly and can only be set via the constructor.

Advantages of Immutability in C#

Thread Safety: Immutable objects can be shared across threads without worrying about synchronization or race conditions.

Predictability: Functions or methods that operate on immutable objects will not alter their inputs, ensuring consistent and predictable behavior.

Simplified Debugging: Since the data does not change over time, it is easier to trace and debug the application's behavior.

Function Composition: Immutability encourages functional programming techniques like function composition, where data is transformed in a series of steps rather than being modified in-place.

Conclusion

Implementing immutability in C# applications is straightforward and brings significant benefits, including safer, more maintainable, and easier-to-debug code. By using techniques such as readonly fields, immutable collections, records, and functional programming patterns, developers can create robust applications that avoid issues associated with mutable state, such as race conditions and unintended side effects.

Chapter 5
Pure Functions and Side Effects

Pure functions are a fundamental concept in functional programming. A pure function is a function that:

Always produces the same output for the same input: The result of the function depends solely on its input parameters, with no reliance on external state or variables.
Has no side effects: It does not modify any external state, such as global variables, files, databases, or user interfaces.

Characteristics of Pure Functions

Deterministic behavior: Input
x
x always gives output
y
y.

No modification of external variables or data.
Easier to test and debug because they are predictable.

Example of a Pure Function in C#:

csharp
Copy code
```csharp
public int Add(int a, int b)
{
    return a + b;
}
```

This function is pure because it always returns the same sum for the same input and does not alter any external state.

What Are Side Effects?

Side effects occur when a function interacts with or modifies external state. This could involve:

Changing a global variable.

Writing to or reading from a file or database.
Modifying input arguments.
Printing to the console or updating a UI.
Example of a Function with Side Effects:

csharp
Copy code

```
public int IncrementCounter()
{
    counter++; // Modifies an external variable
    return counter;
}
```

Here, the function modifies a global variable (counter), making it impure and harder to predict or test.

Why Avoid Side Effects?

Predictability: Pure functions make code easier to understand and reason about.
Reusability: Pure functions are independent and can be reused in different contexts.
Testability: Pure functions are easier to test because they rely only on inputs and outputs, without requiring setup or cleanup of external state.

By writing pure functions and minimizing side effects, developers can create more reliable and maintainable code.

5.1 The Principle of Pure Functions

The principle of pure functions is a cornerstone of functional programming. A pure function is a function that adheres to two key rules:

Deterministic Output: A pure function always produces the same output for the same input. Its behavior is entirely predictable because it depends solely on its input arguments. No Side Effects: A pure function does not cause any changes to the external state or rely on any external data that might change during execution.

This principle promotes code that is predictable, maintainable, and testable, making pure functions an essential tool for clean and reliable programming.

Characteristics of Pure Functions

Deterministic Behavior: A pure function always produces the same result for identical inputs, which ensures consistency and reliability.
State Independence: Pure functions rely only on their input parameters and do not interact with external variables, databases, files, or global state.
Immutability: Pure functions do not modify their inputs or any other external data.

Advantages of Pure Functions

Predictability: Since the output depends only on the input, pure functions are easy to reason about.

Reusability: Pure functions are independent and can be used across different parts of an application without unintended interactions.

Testability: Testing pure functions is straightforward because they do not depend on external factors.

Concurrency-Friendly: Pure functions are inherently thread-safe, as they do not modify shared state.

Examples of Pure Functions in C#
Pure Function:

```csharp
Copy code
public int Add(int a, int b)
{
    return a + b;
}
```

This function is pure because it:

Always returns the same sum for the same inputs.
Does not modify any external variables or state.

Impure Function:

```csharp
Copy code
public int IncrementCounter()
{
    counter++; // Modifies an external variable
    return counter;
}
```

This function is impure because it changes the value of the external variable counter, violating the principle of no side effects.

When to Use Pure Functions
Pure functions are ideal for:

Mathematical computations.
Data transformation (e.g., filtering, mapping, or reducing collections).
Situations requiring predictability and testability.

Challenges of Pure Functions

I/O Operations: Tasks like reading from or writing to a file or database inherently involve side effects, so they cannot be pure.

State Management: Managing state in applications (e.g., updating a user interface) often requires side effects, requiring careful design to balance purity with practicality.

Conclusion

The principle of pure functions is vital for building robust and maintainable software. By focusing on deterministic outputs and eliminating side effects, developers can create code that is easier to debug, test, and reuse. While not all functions in a program can be pure, adhering to this principle wherever possible leads to cleaner and more reliable applications.

5.2 Managing Side Effects in Functional Code

Functional programming emphasizes immutability and pure functions, yet many real-world applications require side effects, such as reading from files, updating databases, or interacting with user interfaces. Managing these side effects effectively is crucial to maintaining the principles of functional programming while accommodating practical needs.

What Are Side Effects?

A side effect occurs when a function interacts with the external world or modifies state outside its scope. Examples include:

Modifying global or shared variables.
Writing to or reading from a file.
Updating a database.
Printing to the console.
Altering user interface elements.

While side effects are unavoidable in certain situations, managing them helps reduce complexity, maintain code predictability, and ensure testability.

Strategies for Managing Side Effects

1. Isolating Side Effects

One common strategy is to isolate side effects in specific parts of the codebase. By separating pure computations from impure operations, you can limit the spread of side effects and keep most of your code functional.

Example:

```csharp
Copy code
public List<int> GetDoubledNumbers(string filePath)
{
    // Side effect: Reading from a file
    var numbers = File.ReadAllLines(filePath).Select(int.Parse).ToList();

    // Pure function: Transforming data
    return numbers.Select(n => n * 2).ToList();
}
```

In this example, the file reading is isolated from the transformation logic, making the computational part pure and testable.

2. Using Functional Wrappers

Functional programming often employs wrappers like monads to encapsulate and manage side effects. For example, in languages like C#, you can use constructs such as Task or Option to represent computations with potential side effects.

Example with Task:

```csharp
Copy code
public async Task<string> FetchDataAsync(string url)
{
    // Side effect: Network request
    var response = await httpClient.GetStringAsync(url);
    return response;
}
```

Here, the Task type encapsulates the side effect of making an HTTP request, making it easier to compose with other functional operations.

3. Dependency Injection

Injecting dependencies, such as services for database access or logging, allows you to control and mock side effects for testing purposes. This approach makes the impure parts of the code modular and easier to manage.

Example:

```csharp
Copy code
public class UserService
{
    private readonly IUserRepository _repository;

    public UserService(IUserRepository repository)
    {
        _repository = repository;
    }

    public User GetUserById(int id)
    {
        // Side effect: Database query
        return _repository.GetUser(id);
    }
}
```

4. Pure Wrappers Around Impure Functions

You can create pure functions that return commands or data structures representing side effects, which can be executed later by an external system.

Example:

csharp
Copy code
```csharp
public Func<string> LogMessage(string message)
{
    // Return a function that logs the message
    return () => { Console.WriteLine(message); return message; };
}
```

This approach separates the description of the side effect from its execution, enabling better control over when and how side effects occur.

5. Using Immutable Data

By keeping data immutable and treating state changes as transformations, you can minimize unintended side effects.

State updates can be handled by creating new versions of data rather than modifying existing data.

Example:

csharp
Copy code
```csharp
public Order UpdateOrderStatus(Order order, string status)
{
    // Create a new instance with updated status
    return new Order(order.Id, status, order.Items);
}
```

6. Batching and Consolidating Side Effects

Batching side effects into a single operation minimizes the number of interactions with external systems, reducing complexity and improving performance.

Example:

csharp
Copy code
```csharp
public void SaveUsers(IEnumerable<User> users)
```

```
{
    // Side effect: Batch database operation
    _dbContext.Users.AddRange(users);
    _dbContext.SaveChanges();
}
```

Best Practices for Managing Side Effects

Keep the Core Pure: Ensure the majority of your codebase remains pure and functional. Encapsulate side effects in clearly defined boundaries.

Minimize Side Effects: Only introduce side effects when absolutely necessary.

Test Separately: Test pure functions independently and mock side effects during testing.

Compose Functions: Use higher-order functions or functional wrappers to compose operations, making them modular and reusable.

Conclusion

Managing side effects in functional code is about balancing purity with practicality. By isolating, encapsulating, and controlling side effects, developers can maintain the benefits of functional programming—such as predictability, testability, and maintainability—while addressing the real-world needs of software systems.

Chapter 6
Closures and Anonymous Functions

Closures and anonymous functions are powerful constructs in functional programming and are widely used in C# to simplify and enhance code flexibility.

Closures

A closure is a function that "closes over" the variables from its surrounding scope, even after that scope has exited. In other words, a closure can capture and use local variables from its enclosing function.

Key Features:

Access to variables in the outer scope.
Maintains the state of those variables even when executed outside their original context.

Example in C#:

```csharp
Copy code
Func<int, int> CreateMultiplier(int factor)
{
    return x => x * factor;  // 'factor' is captured by the
closure
}


var multiplyBy2 = CreateMultiplier(2);
Console.WriteLine(multiplyBy2(5));  // Output: 10
```

Here, the returned lambda function remembers the value of factor even after the CreateMultiplier method has finished executing.

Anonymous Functions

An anonymous function is a function defined without a name. In C#, they are commonly expressed as lambdas or delegate literals. Anonymous functions are typically used for short-lived operations, such as inline event handlers or callbacks.

Key Features:

Concise syntax.

Often used with LINQ, event handlers, or functional operations like map and filter.

Example of an Anonymous Function in C#:

csharp
Copy code
```
var square = (int x) => x * x; // Lambda expression
Console.WriteLine(square(4)); // Output: 16
```

With LINQ:

csharp
Copy code
```
var numbers = new[] { 1, 2, 3, 4 };
var squares = numbers.Select(x => x * x).ToList();
Console.WriteLine(string.Join(", ", squares)); // Output: 1, 4, 9, 16
```

Closures and Anonymous Functions Together

Closures often leverage anonymous functions to retain context from their surrounding scope.

Example:

```csharp
Copy code
int counter = 0;
Func<int> Increment = () => ++counter;  // Closure capturing 'counter'
Console.WriteLine(Increment()); // Output: 1
Console.WriteLine(Increment()); // Output: 2
```

Use Cases

Event Handlers: Inline callbacks for user interaction.
Functional Operations: Used with LINQ methods like Select, Where, and Aggregate.
State Management: Capturing and managing external state in closures.

Closures and anonymous functions simplify coding by making functions more modular, concise, and powerful, particularly in scenarios requiring dynamic or context-aware behavior.

6.1 Understanding Closures in C#

Closures are a core concept in functional programming, enabling functions to "close over" and retain access to variables from their enclosing scope, even after that scope has exited. In C#, closures are often implemented using lambda expressions or anonymous functions.

What Is a Closure?
A closure is created when:

A function is defined within another function or method.

The inner function references variables or parameters from the enclosing function's scope.

Closures "capture" these variables, allowing them to persist beyond the execution of the enclosing function, creating a snapshot of their state at the time of capture.

How Closures Work in C#

In C#, closures are typically created using lambda expressions or delegates. When a lambda expression references variables from the outer scope, it becomes a closure.

Example:

csharp
Copy code
Func<int, int> CreateMultiplier(int factor)
{
    return x => x * factor; // 'factor' is captured by the
closure
}

var multiplyBy3 = CreateMultiplier(3);
Console.WriteLine(multiplyBy3(5)); // Output: 15

Here, the lambda expression x => x * factor captures the factor variable from the outer scope. Even though the CreateMultiplier method has exited, the multiplyBy3 function retains access to the factor variable.

Key Characteristics of Closures

Variable Capture: Closures can capture and store references to local variables or parameters from their enclosing scope.

State Preservation: Captured variables persist as long as the closure exists.

Dynamic Behavior: Closures allow functions to adapt their behavior based on external variables.

Real-World Use Cases of Closures in C#

Deferred Execution: Closures enable lazy evaluation by capturing variables and delaying their use until required.

```csharp
Copy code
List<Func<int>> funcs = new();
for (int i = 0; i < 3; i++)
{
    funcs.Add(() => i); // Captures the loop variable 'i'
}
foreach (var func in funcs)
{
    Console.WriteLine(func()); // Output: 3, 3, 3 (due to shared closure)
}
```

Fixing this issue involves creating a copy of the variable:

```csharp
Copy code
for (int i = 0; i < 3; i++)
{
    int temp = i;  // Create a copy
    funcs.Add(() => temp);
}
foreach (var func in funcs)
{
    Console.WriteLine(func());  // Output: 0, 1, 2
}
```

Event Handlers: Closures simplify capturing state for dynamic event handling.

```csharp
Copy code
for (int i = 0; i < 3; i++)
{
    int temp = i;  // Capture variable
    Button btn = new Button();
    btn.Click += (sender, args) => Console.WriteLine($"Button {temp} clicked");
}
```

Functional Programming Patterns: Used in LINQ queries and higher-order functions.

csharp
Copy code

```
var numbers = new[] { 1, 2, 3, 4 };
int multiplier = 2;
var results = numbers.Select(x => x * multiplier).ToList();
Console.WriteLine(string.Join(", ", results)); // Output: 2, 4, 6, 8
```

Advantages of Closures

Simplifies Code: Reduces boilerplate by capturing and preserving state automatically.
Improves Flexibility: Allows functions to adapt dynamically to context-specific variables.
Enhances Modularity: Enables creating reusable and self-contained code blocks.

Caveats of Using Closures

Unintended Captures: Shared closures may lead to unexpected behavior (e.g., in loops).

Memory Leaks: Captured variables can extend the lifetime of objects, potentially causing memory issues.

Complex Debugging: Closures add layers of abstraction, making debugging more challenging.

Conclusion

Closures are a powerful tool in C#, enabling functions to maintain access to variables from their enclosing scope. By understanding how closures work and their potential pitfalls, developers can leverage them to write concise, flexible, and dynamic code for a wide range of scenarios.

6.2 Using Lambdas and Anonymous Functions Effectively

In C#, lambdas and anonymous functions are indispensable tools for writing clean, concise, and expressive code. They allow developers to define short-lived functions inline without requiring a formal method declaration, making code more modular and easier to understand.

Understanding Lambdas and Anonymous Functions

Anonymous Functions: Functions without a name. In C#, anonymous functions can be represented using:

Lambda expressions (modern syntax).
Anonymous methods (legacy syntax, less common).
Lambda Expressions: A concise syntax for defining anonymous functions using the => operator. They are widely used in LINQ queries, event handling, and functional programming patterns.

Example of a Lambda:

```csharp
Copy code
Func<int, int> square = x => x * x;
Console.WriteLine(square(5)); // Output: 25
```

Example of an Anonymous Method:

```csharp
```

```
Copy code
Func<int, int> square = delegate (int x) { return x * x;
};
Console.WriteLine(square(5));  // Output: 25
```

Effective Use Cases for Lambdas and Anonymous Functions

Simplifying LINQ Queries Lambdas are integral to LINQ, enabling concise query definitions.

```csharp
Copy code
var numbers = new[] { 1, 2, 3, 4 };
var squares = numbers.Select(x => x * x).ToList();
Console.WriteLine(string.Join(", ", squares));     //
Output: 1, 4, 9, 16
```

Event Handling Lambdas allow inline event handlers without needing separate methods.

```csharp
Copy code
Button button = new Button();
```

button.Click += (sender, args) => Console.WriteLine("Button clicked!");

Higher-Order Functions Use lambdas to pass functions as arguments or return functions.

csharp
Copy code

```csharp
Func<int, Func<int, int>> CreateAdder = x => y => x + y;
var add5 = CreateAdder(5);
Console.WriteLine(add5(10)); // Output: 15
```

Callbacks Lambdas are ideal for defining short callback functions.

csharp
Copy code

```csharp
Task.Run(() => Console.WriteLine("Task completed!"));
```

Custom Sorting Lambdas simplify custom sorting logic.

csharp
Copy code

```csharp
var names = new[] { "Alice", "Bob", "Charlie" };
```

```csharp
var sortedNames = names.OrderBy(name =>
name.Length).ToList();
Console.WriteLine(string.Join(", ", sortedNames)); //
Output: Bob, Alice, Charlie
```

Tips for Using Lambdas and Anonymous Functions
Effectively

.

Keep Lambdas Short and Focused

Avoid complex logic in lambdas. Extract larger logic into
named methods for readability.
csharp
Copy code
```csharp
var evenNumbers = numbers.Where(x => x % 2 ==
0).ToList(); // Simple and clear
```

Use Type Inference

Let the compiler infer types to reduce verbosity.
csharp
Copy code
```csharp
var result = numbers.Select(x => x * x); // No need to
specify 'int' explicitly
```

Avoid Repetition

Use lambdas with higher-order functions to eliminate repetitive code.

csharp
Copy code
```csharp
void ProcessList(List<int> list, Func<int, int> operation)
{
    list.ForEach(item => Console.WriteLine(operation(item)));
}
ProcessList(numbers, x => x * 2);
```

Leverage Closures

Capture variables from the enclosing scope to dynamically alter lambda behavior.

csharp
Copy code
```csharp
int multiplier = 3;
var tripled = numbers.Select(x => x * multiplier).ToList();
```

Handle Side Effects Carefully

Avoid introducing unnecessary side effects in lambdas to maintain functional purity.

csharp
Copy code

```csharp
numbers.ForEach(x => Console.WriteLine(x));    // Simple output, no state changes
```

Debug with Care

Use descriptive variables and comments to clarify intent when lambdas are used in complex logic.

csharp
Copy code

```csharp
var expensiveItems = items.Where(item =>
{
    // Filter items over $100
    return item.Price > 100;
}).ToList();
```

Advantages of Using Lambdas and Anonymous Functions

Conciseness: Reduces boilerplate, making code more compact.

Modularity: Encourages functional programming principles like immutability and statelessness.

Dynamic Behavior: Easily pass or return custom logic for dynamic use cases.

Improved Readability: When used properly, lambdas make code more expressive and understandable.

Potential Pitfalls and How to Avoid Them

Overuse Leading to Complexity

Complex lambdas can obscure logic. Break them into smaller named functions when needed.

Unintended Closures

Ensure captured variables are correctly scoped to avoid bugs in loops or asynchronous operations.

Readability Challenges

Use clear, descriptive names for variables and keep lambdas simple to maintain clarity.

Conclusion

Lambdas and anonymous functions are powerful tools that, when used effectively, improve code modularity, readability, and maintainability. By leveraging their concise syntax and functional capabilities, C# developers can write expressive and efficient code tailored to modern programming challenges.

PART III: ADVANCED FUNCTIONAL PROGRAMMING TECHNIQUES

Chapter 7
Working with LINQ for Functional Programming

Language-Integrated Query (LINQ) is a powerful feature in C# that supports functional programming by enabling declarative and concise data manipulation. It abstracts complex iterations and transformations, allowing developers to process collections with ease while focusing on what needs to be done rather than how to do it.

Key Features of LINQ in Functional Programming

Declarative Syntax: LINQ uses a high-level, SQL-like syntax to describe operations on data.
Immutability: LINQ methods return new collections without modifying the original, promoting immutability.
First-Class Functions: LINQ works seamlessly with lambda expressions, allowing developers to pass functions as arguments for queries.

Common LINQ Methods for Functional Programming

Where: Filters elements based on a predicate.

csharp
Copy code
var evenNumbers = numbers.Where(x => x % 2 == 0);

Select: Projects each element into a new form.

csharp
Copy code
var squares = numbers.Select(x => x * x);

Aggregate: Reduces a sequence into a single value.

csharp
Copy code
var sum = numbers.Aggregate((acc, x) => acc + x);

GroupBy: Groups elements based on a key selector.

csharp
Copy code
var grouped = people.GroupBy(p => p.Age);

OrderBy/OrderByDescending: Sorts elements in ascending or descending order.

csharp

Copy code

var sorted = names.OrderBy(name => name.Length);

Functional Programming Benefits of LINQ

Readable Code: Simplifies data transformations by chaining methods, reducing boilerplate.

Immutability: Encourages functional paradigms by returning new collections.

Compact and Expressive: Allows complex queries to be written succinctly.

Example: Combining LINQ Methods

csharp

Copy code

```
var employees = new[]
{
    new { Name = "Alice", Salary = 50000 },
    new { Name = "Bob", Salary = 70000 },
    new { Name = "Charlie", Salary = 60000 }
};
```

```
var highEarners = employees
  .Where(e => e.Salary > 55000)
  .OrderByDescending(e => e.Salary)
  .Select(e => e.Name);

Console.WriteLine(string.Join(", ", highEarners));   // Output: Bob, Charlie
```

Conclusion

LINQ integrates functional programming principles into C# by enabling declarative, efficient, and immutable operations on data. By leveraging LINQ's powerful methods, developers can write cleaner, more maintainable, and expressive code for data processing tasks.

7.1 LINQ as a Functional Paradigm in C#

Language Integrated Query (LINQ) in C# is a core feature that embodies the principles of functional programming. By providing a declarative and composable way to query and manipulate data, LINQ promotes immutability, stateless operations, and higher-order functions, which are fundamental to functional paradigms. LINQ seamlessly integrates with collections, databases, XML, and more, making it a versatile tool for developers.

Functional Principles in LINQ

Declarative Syntax
LINQ emphasizes what to do rather than how to do it, abstracting away iterative details.

```csharp
Copy code
var evenNumbers = numbers.Where(n => n % 2 == 0);
```

Immutability

LINQ operations, such as filtering or projecting, return new collections without altering the original data source, encouraging immutability.

csharp
Copy code

**var squaredNumbers = numbers.Select(n => n * n); //
Original 'numbers' remains unchanged.**

Higher-Order Functions

LINQ methods accept functions (e.g., predicates or
projections) as arguments, making it a natural fit for
functional programming.

Chaining

LINQ queries support method chaining, allowing for
concise and modular transformations.

csharp
Copy code
```csharp
var sortedNames = names
  .Where(name => name.Length > 3)
  .OrderBy(name => name)
  .ToList();
```

Key Functional Concepts Enabled by LINQ

Filtering
Use Where to filter elements based on conditions.

csharp

Copy code

var adults = people.Where(p => p.Age >= 18);

Projection

Use Select to transform elements into a new form.

csharp

Copy code

var names = people.Select(p => p.Name);

Reduction

Use Aggregate to reduce a collection to a single value.

csharp

Copy code

var sum = numbers.Aggregate((total, n) => total + n);

Sorting

Use OrderBy and OrderByDescending for ordering collections.

csharp
Copy code
```csharp
var ordered = names.OrderBy(name => name.Length);
```

Grouping

Use GroupBy to group elements based on a key.

csharp
Copy code
```csharp
var groups = people.GroupBy(p => p.AgeGroup);
```

Composition

LINQ's method chaining allows combining multiple operations efficiently.

csharp
Copy code
```csharp
var result = products
    .Where(p => p.Price > 100)
    .OrderBy(p => p.Name)
    .Select(p => new { p.Name, p.Price });
```

Benefits of LINQ as a Functional Paradigm

Readability: Declarative syntax simplifies complex data processing logic.

Reusability: Encapsulates logic into composable queries.

Modularity: Each LINQ method focuses on a specific operation.

Testability: Immutability and statelessness improve testability by avoiding side effects.

Example: LINQ Query in Action

```csharp
Copy code
var employees = new[]
{
    new { Name = "Alice", Age = 30, Salary = 50000 },
    new { Name = "Bob", Age = 40, Salary = 70000 },
    new { Name = "Charlie", Age = 35, Salary = 60000 }
};

var highEarners = employees
    .Where(e => e.Salary > 55000)
    .OrderByDescending(e => e.Salary)
```

```
.Select(e => e.Name);

Console.WriteLine(string.Join(",  ",  highEarners));  //
Output: Bob, Charlie
```

Conclusion

LINQ serves as a bridge between traditional imperative programming and functional paradigms in C#. Its declarative style, support for higher-order functions, immutability, and composability make it a powerful tool for applying functional programming principles. By leveraging LINQ, developers can write clean, maintainable, and efficient code for modern software development.

7.2 Advanced LINQ Queries and Transformations

LINQ (Language Integrated Query) is a powerful tool in C# that allows developers to query and manipulate collections, databases, and other data sources in a declarative manner. While basic LINQ operations like Where, Select, and

OrderBy are essential, advanced LINQ queries unlock the full potential of LINQ for more complex data transformations and manipulation tasks. These advanced operations can significantly simplify data workflows and enhance code readability.

1. Grouping Data

Grouping is one of the most powerful features of LINQ. The GroupBy method allows you to categorize data into groups based on a specified key. This is useful for organizing data before applying further transformations.

Example:

Grouping a list of employees by their department:

csharp
Copy code
```csharp
var employees = new[]
{
    new { Name = "Alice", Department = "HR", Salary = 50000 },
    new { Name = "Bob", Department = "IT", Salary = 70000 },
    new { Name = "Charlie", Department = "IT", Salary = 60000 },
```

```csharp
    new { Name = "David", Department = "HR", Salary
= 55000 }
};

var groupedByDepartment = employees
  .GroupBy(e => e.Department)
  .Select(group => new
  {
    Department = group.Key,
    Employees = group.ToList()
  });

foreach (var group in groupedByDepartment)
{
  Console.WriteLine(group.Department);
  foreach (var employee in group.Employees)
  {
          Console.WriteLine($"    {employee.Name},
{employee.Salary}");
  }
}
```

2. Aggregating Data

Aggregation operations like Sum, Average, Min, Max, and Aggregate allow you to perform calculations on data.

Example:
Calculating the total salary of all employees:

csharp
Copy code
```
var totalSalary = employees
    .Sum(e => e.Salary);
Console.WriteLine($"Total Salary: {totalSalary}");
```

Example with Aggregate:

You can also use Aggregate for custom reductions.

csharp
Copy code
```
var totalSalaryUsingAggregate = employees
    .Aggregate(0, (acc, e) => acc + e.Salary);
Console.WriteLine($"Total Salary Using Aggregate: {totalSalaryUsingAggregate}");
```

3. Joining Data

Joining is a fundamental operation when working with multiple collections. LINQ supports several types of joins such as inner joins, outer joins, and group joins.

Example: Inner Join
Joining two collections based on a common key:

```csharp
Copy code
var departments = new[]
{
    new { DepartmentId = 1, DepartmentName = "HR" },
    new { DepartmentId = 2, DepartmentName = "IT" }
};

var employeeDepartments = from e in employees
            join d in departments on e.Department equals d.DepartmentName
            select new
            {
                e.Name,
                e.Salary,
                d.DepartmentName
            };
```

```csharp
foreach (var item in employeeDepartments)
{
        Console.WriteLine($"{item.Name} works in {item.DepartmentName} with salary {item.Salary}");
}
```

Example: Left Join (using DefaultIfEmpty for outer join)

csharp
Copy code
```csharp
var leftJoin = from e in employees
        join d in departments on e.Department equals d.DepartmentName into deptGroup
        from dept in deptGroup.DefaultIfEmpty()
        select new
        {
           e.Name,
                            DepartmentName = dept?.DepartmentName ?? "Unknown"
        };

foreach (var item in leftJoin)
{
```

```csharp
        Console.WriteLine($"{item.Name}   works   in
{item.DepartmentName}");
}
```

4. Nested Queries

LINQ allows the use of nested queries to operate on collections within collections. This is useful when dealing with more complex data structures.

Example:
Selecting employees with salaries greater than the average salary:

```csharp
csharp
Copy code
var avgSalary = employees.Average(e => e.Salary);
var highEarners = employees
   .Where(e => e.Salary > avgSalary)
   .Select(e => new { e.Name, e.Salary });

foreach (var employee in highEarners)
{
        Console.WriteLine($"{employee.Name}   earns
{employee.Salary}");
```

}

5. Projection with Anonymous Types

LINQ allows you to project data into new shapes using anonymous types. This can be useful when you want to return only a subset of properties or perform transformations on the data.

Example:

Projecting a custom view of employee data:

```csharp
Copy code
var employeeSummary = employees
  .Select(e => new
  {
    e.Name,
    SalaryBracket = e.Salary > 60000 ? "High" : "Low"
  });

foreach (var item in employeeSummary)
{
```

```csharp
            Console.WriteLine($"{item.Name}:
{item.SalaryBracket} salary");
}
```

6. Ordering Data with Multiple Criteria

LINQ allows sorting by multiple criteria using method chaining, providing a flexible approach for complex sorting operations.

Example:
Sorting employees first by department and then by salary:

```csharp
csharp
Copy code
var sortedEmployees = employees
   .OrderBy(e => e.Department)
   .ThenByDescending(e => e.Salary);

foreach (var employee in sortedEmployees)
{
            Console.WriteLine($"{employee.Name}    -
{employee.Department} - {employee.Salary}");
}
```

7. Using SelectMany for Flattening Collections

The SelectMany method is a powerful tool for flattening collections. It is used when you have a collection of collections and want to combine them into a single sequence.

Example:
Flattening a collection of employee projects:

```csharp
Copy code
var employeeProjects = new[]
{
    new { Employee = "Alice", Projects = new[] { "Project1", "Project2" } },
    new { Employee = "Bob", Projects = new[] { "Project3", "Project4" } }
};

var allProjects = employeeProjects
    .SelectMany(e => e.Projects)
    .ToList();
```

```
foreach (var project in allProjects)
{
    Console.WriteLine(project);
}
```

8. Combining LINQ with Other Functional Concepts

LINQ's integration with C# functional features allows you to combine advanced functional programming patterns, such as lazy evaluation, higher-order functions, and immutability.

Example:
Using Func and Action delegates with LINQ:

csharp
Copy code
```
Func<int, bool> isEven = n => n % 2 == 0;
var evenNumbers = numbers.Where(isEven);

Action<int> print = n => Console.WriteLine(n);
evenNumbers.ToList().ForEach(print);
```

Conclusion

Advanced LINQ queries and transformations provide a robust, functional approach to data processing in C#. By leveraging LINQ's powerful methods—such as GroupBy, Aggregate, Join, and SelectMany—developers can build efficient, clean, and expressive data manipulation pipelines. These techniques support the principles of functional programming, such as immutability, higher-order functions, and declarative logic, making LINQ a fundamental tool for advanced data transformation tasks.

Chapter 8
Pattern Matching and Deconstruction

Pattern matching is a feature in C# that allows you to test and extract values from objects in a concise and readable way. It enables you to match types, values, and properties, simplifying the code and making it more expressive. Pattern matching was enhanced in C# 7.0 and further improved in C# 9.0 and later, allowing for more powerful matching scenarios.

Pattern Matching

Pattern matching allows for conditional checks, which make it easier to test an object's type and extract data. It can be used in switch statements, is expressions, and match expressions.

Example of Type Pattern Matching:

csharp
Copy code
```
object obj = "Hello, C#!";

if (obj is string s)
```

```
{
    Console.WriteLine(s); // Output: Hello, C#!
}
```

Here, the is keyword checks the type of obj and, if it matches, assigns it to s.

Example of Switch Expression:

```csharp
Copy code
var result = obj switch
{
    int i => $"Integer: {i}",
    string s => $"String: {s}",
    _ => "Unknown"
};
Console.WriteLine(result);   // Output: String: Hello, C#!
```

Deconstruction

Deconstruction is the process of breaking down an object into its constituent parts. C# allows you to deconstruct objects, typically tuples or user-defined types, into separate variables for easier access.

Example of Deconstruction with Tuples:

```csharp
Copy code
var person = (Name: "Alice", Age: 30);
var (name, age) = person;
Console.WriteLine($"{name}, {age}");  // Output: Alice, 30
```

Example of Deconstructing a Custom Class:

```csharp
Copy code
public class Point
{
    public int X { get; }
    public int Y { get; }

    public Point(int x, int y) => (X, Y) = (x, y);

    public void Deconstruct(out int x, out int y) => (x, y) = (X, Y);
}
```

```csharp
var point = new Point(3, 4);
var (x, y) = point;
Console.WriteLine($"{x}, {y}");  // Output: 3, 4
```

Benefits of Pattern Matching and Deconstruction

Concise Code: Reduces boilerplate code, improving readability and maintainability.

Type Safety: Ensures type correctness at compile-time, reducing runtime errors.

Enhanced Flow Control: Simplifies conditional logic by combining multiple checks into a single expression.

Immutability: Encourages immutability in deconstruction, as it allows easy extraction of values without modifying the original object.

Pattern matching and deconstruction are powerful tools in C# that allow you to work with objects and data more intuitively and efficiently.

8.1 Exploring Pattern Matching in C#

Pattern matching in C# is a powerful feature introduced in C# 7.0 and enhanced in later versions to provide a more concise and expressive way to handle conditional logic and extract data from objects. It allows developers to test an object's type or structure, decompose it into its constituent parts, and apply specific logic based on patterns, all in a clean and readable manner.

1. What is Pattern Matching?

Pattern matching enables developers to test data structures or values against specific patterns and apply logic based on the results. Patterns can be used to:

Check for null values.
Test an object's type.
Extract values from properties or fields.
Combine multiple conditions.

It simplifies common tasks such as type casting, null checks, and conditional branching.

2. Types of Patterns

C# provides several pattern types that can be used in is expressions, switch expressions, and if statements:

a. Constant Pattern

Tests if a value matches a constant:

```csharp
Copy code
int x = 10;
if (x is 10)
{
    Console.WriteLine("x is 10");
}
```

b. Type Pattern
Checks an object's type and, if successful, assigns it to a new variable:

```csharp
Copy code
object obj = "Hello, Pattern Matching!";
if (obj is string str)
{
    Console.WriteLine($"String value: {str}");
```

```
}
```

c. Relational Pattern (C# 9.0+)

Compares a value against relational operators:

```
csharp
Copy code
int age = 25;
if (age is > 18 and < 30)
{
    Console.WriteLine("Age is between 18 and 30");
}
```

d. Logical Pattern (C# 9.0+)

Combines patterns using and, or, and not keywords:

```
csharp
Copy code
int value = 15;
if (value is > 10 and not 20)
{
    Console.WriteLine("Value is greater than 10 but not 20");
```

}

e. Property Pattern

Matches objects based on the values of their properties:

```csharp
Copy code
var person = new { Name = "Alice", Age = 25 };
if (person is { Age: > 20 })
{
    Console.WriteLine("Person is older than 20");
}
```

f. Positional Pattern (C# 8.0+)

Decomposes objects using their deconstructor method:

```csharp
Copy code
var point = new Point(3, 4);
if (point is (3, 4))
{
    Console.WriteLine("Point is at (3, 4)");
}
```

```csharp
// Example Class
public class Point
{
    public int X { get; }
    public int Y { get; }
    public Point(int x, int y) => (X, Y) = (x, y);
    public void Deconstruct(out int x, out int y) => (x, y) = (X, Y);
}
```

3. Pattern Matching with switch Expressions

The switch statement in C# has been modernized to use patterns, reducing the need for verbose conditional blocks.

Example: Type Pattern in switch Expression

csharp
Copy code
```csharp
object data = 42;

var result = data switch
{
    int i => $"Integer: {i}",
    string s => $"String: {s}",
```

```
    null => "Null value",
    _ => "Unknown type"
};
Console.WriteLine(result);
```

Example: Property Pattern in switch Expression

csharp

Copy code

```csharp
var person = new { Name = "Alice", Age = 25 };

var category = person switch
{
    { Age: < 18 } => "Child",
    { Age: >= 18 and < 65 } => "Adult",
    { Age: >= 65 } => "Senior",
    _ => "Unknown"
};
Console.WriteLine(category);
```

4. Combining Patterns for Complex Scenarios

Patterns can be combined to handle sophisticated logic while keeping the code concise.

Example:

csharp
Copy code
```
object obj = new { Name = "Alice", Age = 25 };

if (obj is { Name: "Alice", Age: > 20 })
{
    Console.WriteLine("Alice is older than 20");
}
```

5. Benefits of Pattern Matching

Improved Code Readability: Reduces the need for repetitive casting and null checks.

Type Safety: Ensures that type checks and assignments are verified at compile-time.

Declarative Logic: Expresses complex conditions in a clear, compact form.

Versatility: Works with a wide range of data types, including custom objects, tuples, and collections.

6. Practical Applications

Simplifying type checks and conversions.

Extracting specific properties or fields from objects.

Replacing verbose if-else or switch blocks.

Implementing data validation or transformation logic.

Conclusion

Pattern matching in C# has evolved into a versatile feature that simplifies the way developers handle conditional logic and data extraction. By leveraging its powerful capabilities—such as type patterns, property patterns, and logical patterns—developers can write cleaner, more expressive, and maintainable code, fully embracing the functional programming principles within C#.

8.2 Using Deconstruction for Simplified Code

Deconstruction in C# is a feature that allows objects or data structures to be broken down into their constituent parts and assigned to separate variables in a single operation.

Introduced in C# 7.0 and enhanced in later versions, deconstruction simplifies code, improves readability, and reduces boilerplate by providing a clean way to work with complex objects or tuples.

What is Deconstruction?

Deconstruction is the process of unpacking the elements of an object or a tuple into individual variables. It allows you to work with data in a more intuitive way, especially when dealing with composite objects or tuples.

Example: Deconstructing a Tuple

csharp
Copy code
```
var person = ("Alice", 30);
(string name, int age) = person;

Console.WriteLine($"{name}, {age}"); // Output: Alice, 30
```

Deconstructing Custom Types

Custom types can also support deconstruction by implementing a

Deconstruct method. This method defines how the object's fields or properties should be broken down.

Example:

```csharp
Copy code
public class Point
{
    public int X { get; }
    public int Y { get; }

    public Point(int x, int y) => (X, Y) = (x, y);

    public void Deconstruct(out int x, out int y) => (x, y) = (X, Y);
}

var point = new Point(5, 10);
var (x, y) = point;
```

Console.WriteLine($"X: {x}, Y: {y}"); // Output: X: 5, Y: 10

Deconstruction in Methods

Deconstruction can be used in method parameters and return values to simplify interactions with complex data.

Returning Tuples and Deconstructing

```csharp
Copy code
(string name, int age) GetPerson() => ("Bob", 40);

var (name, age) = GetPerson();
Console.WriteLine($"{name}, {age}"); // Output: Bob, 40
```

Deconstruction in foreach Loops

Deconstruction can be used in foreach loops to simplify iteration over collections of tuples or objects.

Example:

```csharp
csharp
Copy code
var points = new List<(int X, int Y)>
{
    (1, 2),
    (3, 4),
    (5, 6)
};

foreach (var (x, y) in points)
{
    Console.WriteLine($"X: {x}, Y: {y}");
}
```

Advantages of Using Deconstruction

Code Readability: Simplifies access to multiple values, making the code easier to read and maintain.

Reduced Boilerplate: Removes the need for verbose field or property extraction logic.

Functional Style: Aligns with functional programming practices by treating data as immutable and separating it into components.

141

Versatility: Works seamlessly with tuples, records, and custom types.

Practical Use Cases

Data Parsing: Extracting key-value pairs or elements from a tuple or structured object.

Simplified Method Interactions: Passing and receiving multiple values through concise syntax.

Iteration Over Complex Data: Navigating collections with multiple attributes (e.g., coordinates, key-value pairs).

Domain-Specific Applications: Simplifying the handling of mathematical or geometric objects like vectors and points.

Conclusion

Deconstruction is a practical feature in C# that significantly reduces complexity when working with composite data. By allowing tuples, objects, and custom types to be split into smaller parts, deconstruction enhances code readability, reduces verbosity, and encourages functional programming principles. It's a valuable tool for any developer looking to write more expressive and efficient code.

Chapter 9
Functional Data Structures

Functional data structures are immutable structures that align with the principles of functional programming. Instead of modifying an existing structure, operations on these data structures create new versions while preserving the original, ensuring immutability and thread safety. These data structures are particularly useful in scenarios where immutability and concurrency are key requirements.

Characteristics of Functional Data Structures

Immutability: Once created, the data cannot be changed. Any modification produces a new structure.

Persistent: Previous versions of the structure remain accessible after updates.

Structural Sharing: Instead of duplicating the entire structure during updates, unchanged parts are reused, optimizing memory and performance.

Thread-Safe: Because data is immutable, multiple threads can safely access the same structure without synchronization.

Examples of Functional Data Structures

Lists: Immutable linked lists, such as System.Collections.Immutable.ImmutableList in C#, provide efficient element addition and retrieval.
Trees: Immutable binary trees or tries are used for hierarchical data storage, with updates creating new paths while sharing unmodified branches.
Maps and Sets: Persistent maps and sets maintain immutability while allowing efficient lookup, insertion, and deletion.

Advantages

Predictable Behavior: Avoids side effects and makes reasoning about code easier.
Thread Safety: Ideal for concurrent programming.
Easy Undo/Redo: Previous states can be retrieved effortlessly.

Example in C#

Using System.Collections.Immutable for immutable data structures:

```csharp
Copy code
using System.Collections.Immutable;

var list = ImmutableList<int>.Empty;
var newList = list.Add(1).Add(2);

Console.WriteLine(string.Join(", ", newList)); // Output: 1, 2
Console.WriteLine(string.Join(", ", list));   // Output: (unchanged)
```

Conclusion

Functional data structures are foundational to functional programming, promoting immutability, safety, and clarity in code. They are increasingly important in modern software development, especially in multithreaded and distributed environments.

9.1 Functional Lists, Sets, and Maps in C#

Functional programming in C# is supported by immutable data structures like functional lists, sets, and maps. These structures align with functional principles such as immutability and persistence, ensuring thread safety and predictability while improving code clarity.

The System.Collections.Immutable namespace in .NET provides efficient implementations of these functional collections. These collections allow developers to perform operations without altering the original data structure, instead creating new versions with structural sharing to optimize memory usage.

1. Functional Lists

A functional list is an immutable collection that allows operations such as adding or removing items without modifying the original list.

Key Features:

Immutability: Any operation creates a new list.
Persistence: Old versions of the list remain accessible.
Structural Sharing: Reuses parts of the list to optimize memory.

Example:

```csharp
Copy code
using System.Collections.Immutable;

var list = ImmutableList<int>.Empty;
var updatedList = list.Add(1).Add(2).Add(3);

Console.WriteLine(string.Join(", ", updatedList)); // Output: 1, 2, 3
Console.WriteLine(string.Join(", ", list));     // Output: (unchanged)
```

2. Functional Sets

A functional set represents an immutable collection of unique items. Functional sets ensure no duplicates and provide efficient operations like union, intersection, and difference.

Key Features:

Immutable: Operations like adding or removing elements create a new set.
Efficient Operations: Provides high-performance algorithms for set operations.
Thread-Safe: Ideal for concurrent environments.

Example:

```csharp
Copy code
using System.Collections.Immutable;

var set = ImmutableHashSet<int>.Empty;
var updatedSet = set.Add(10).Add(20).Add(30);

Console.WriteLine(string.Join(", ", updatedSet)); // Output: 10, 20, 30
```

Console.WriteLine(string.Join(", ", set));   //
Output: (unchanged)

3. Functional Maps

A functional map (or dictionary) is an immutable collection of key-value pairs. It allows efficient lookups, additions, and updates without mutating the original map.

Key Features:

Immutability: Any modification produces a new map.
Persistence: Previous versions remain intact.
Structural Sharing: Optimized memory usage.

Example:
csharp
Copy code
using System.Collections.Immutable;

var map = ImmutableDictionary<string, int>.Empty;
var updatedMap = map.Add("Alice", 25).Add("Bob", 30);

```
Console.WriteLine(updatedMap["Alice"]);  //  Output:
25
Console.WriteLine(map.ContainsKey("Alice"));       //
Output: False (original map is unchanged)
```

Benefits of Functional Collections

Thread Safety: Immutable collections are inherently safe for multithreaded environments.

Predictable Behavior: No side effects, making debugging easier.

Memory Optimization: Structural sharing reduces memory usage during updates.

Simplifies State Management: Old states are preserved, enabling undo/redo functionality.

Practical Use Cases

Concurrent Programming: Safe to use across threads without locking mechanisms.

Caching: Maintain snapshots of data without overwriting.

Functional Programming: Perfect for building pipelines that transform data immutably.

.Conclusion

Functional lists, sets, and maps in C# enable developers to write clean, thread-safe, and functional-style code.

By leveraging the immutable collections in the System.Collections.Immutable namespace, developers can embrace functional programming principles while benefiting from efficient and optimized operations. These data structures are vital tools for modern software development.

9.2 Designing Efficient Immutable Data Structures

Immutable data structures are critical to functional programming as they guarantee immutability, enabling thread safety, predictable behavior, and simpler debugging. However, designing them efficiently requires overcoming challenges related to performance and memory usage, as every update creates a new structure. To address these challenges, techniques like structural sharing and persistent data structures are employed.

Key Principles of Designing Immutable Data Structures

Immutability: Once created, the structure cannot be modified. Operations on the structure return a new version.
Structural Sharing: Unchanged portions of the data structure are reused between versions to reduce duplication and optimize memory.
Persistence: Previous versions of the data structure remain accessible after updates, supporting undo/redo operations and historical state tracking.
Efficiency: Focus on minimizing the overhead of immutability by designing operations like updates, lookups, and traversals to be fast and memory-efficient.

Techniques for Efficient Immutable Structures

1. Structural Sharing

Structural sharing ensures that only the modified parts of a data structure are copied, while the rest is reused. This minimizes the memory and computational overhead.

Example: Immutable Tree

When adding a node to a binary tree, only the affected path is updated, while the rest of the tree is shared with the new version.

```csharp
Copy code
public class ImmutableNode
{
    public int Value { get; }
    public ImmutableNode? Left { get; }
    public ImmutableNode? Right { get; }

    public ImmutableNode(int value, ImmutableNode? left = null, ImmutableNode? right = null)
    {
        Value = value;
        Left = left;
        Right = right;
    }
```

```
public ImmutableNode Add(int value) =>
    value < Value
        ? new ImmutableNode(Value, Left?.Add(value)
?? new ImmutableNode(value), Right)
            : new ImmutableNode(Value, Left,
Right?.Add(value) ?? new ImmutableNode(value));
}
```

2. Persistent Data Structures

A persistent data structure maintains previous versions of itself even after updates, enabling historical tracking without duplicating the entire structure. Examples include persistent lists, hash maps, and trees.

3. Optimized Algorithms

Efficient immutable data structures rely on algorithms that minimize the cost of updates:

Path Copying: Only the path to the modified element is copied.
Hash Array Mapped Trie (HAMT): Used in functional maps and sets for efficient lookup and update operations.

Immutable Collections in .NET

The System.Collections.Immutable namespace provides efficient implementations of immutable data structures, including:

ImmutableList: A list with structural sharing.

ImmutableHashSet: A set optimized for immutability.
ImmutableDictionary: A key-value pair collection using HAMT for efficiency.

Example: Using ImmutableList

```csharp
Copy code
using System.Collections.Immutable;

var list = ImmutableList<int>.Empty;
var updatedList = list.Add(1).Add(2).Add(3);

Console.WriteLine(string.Join(", ", updatedList)); // Output: 1, 2, 3
Console.WriteLine(string.Join(", ", list));        // Original list remains unchanged
```

Benefits of Efficient Immutable Data Structures

Thread Safety: Immutable structures are naturally thread-safe, as they cannot be altered once created.

Simpler Debugging: Since data doesn't change, debugging is easier with predictable and reproducible states.

State Management: Retaining previous states allows for features like undo/redo, historical tracking, and time-travel debugging.

Functional Compatibility: Immutable structures align seamlessly with functional programming paradigms.

Challenges in Designing Immutable Data Structures

Performance Overhead: Naive implementations may incur high memory and computational costs.

Complexity of Sharing: Implementing structural sharing and persistence can be intricate.

Adoption: Developers accustomed to mutable structures may find the paradigm shift challenging.

Conclusion

Designing efficient immutable data structures requires careful attention to memory optimization, performance, and usability. By leveraging structural sharing, persistent techniques, and modern algorithms, developers can create immutable structures that balance efficiency and functionality. These structures are indispensable in modern programming, particularly for applications demanding high concurrency, predictability, and immutability.

PART IV: HANDLING COMPLEXITY IN FUNCTIONAL PROGRAMMING

Chapter 10
Error Handling with Functional Paradigms

Functional programming emphasizes pure functions and immutable state, which influence how errors are handled. Instead of relying on traditional mechanisms like exceptions, functional paradigms often use explicit and predictable error-handling approaches, such as monads, pattern matching, and result types, to ensure code clarity and composability.

Key Concepts in Functional Error Handling

Immutability and Transparency: Errors are represented as data and handled explicitly, avoiding side effects.
Result Types: Commonly used types like Option or Result encapsulate success or failure, making error handling part of the function's return value.
Composability: Functional error-handling constructs allow chaining operations seamlessly, improving readability and reducing boilerplate code.

Error-Handling Constructs

Option/Maybe Type: Represents a value that may or may not exist.

csharp
Copy code
```
// Example: Using nullable types to represent absence
int? FindValue(int key) => key > 0 ? key : (int?)null;
```

Result/Either Type: Encapsulates success (Ok) or failure (Error), explicitly differentiating outcomes.

csharp
Copy code
```
public class Result<T>
{
    public T? Value { get; }
    public string? Error { get; }
    public bool IsSuccess => Error == null;

    private Result(T value) => Value = value;
    private Result(string error) => Error = error;
```

```csharp
    public static Result<T> Success(T value) =>
new(value);
    public static Result<T> Failure(string error) =>
new(error);
}
```

Pattern Matching: Handles errors in a declarative and concise manner.

```csharp
csharp
Copy code
var result = ProcessData(input);
switch (result)
{
    case Success(var data): HandleSuccess(data); break;
    case Failure(var error): HandleError(error); break;
}
```

Monadic Error Handling: Chains operations and propagates errors without manual checks.

```csharp
csharp
Copy code
var result = input
    .Map(Validate)
```

```
.FlatMap(Process)
.Map(SaveData);
```

Advantages of Functional Error Handling

Predictability: Errors are part of the function's output, making behavior explicit and testable.

Composability: Error-handling constructs integrate seamlessly into functional pipelines.

Readability: Reduces the need for nested error-handling logic, simplifying code.

Conclusion

Error handling in functional paradigms focuses on explicit, predictable, and composable methods. By leveraging constructs like result types, pattern matching, and monads, developers can write more robust and maintainable code while adhering to functional principles.

10.1 Nullables, Optionals, and the Maybe Pattern

Handling the absence of values is a fundamental challenge in programming. Null references, introduced in many imperative languages, often lead to runtime errors such as NullReferenceException. Functional programming offers safer and more expressive alternatives, such as nullables, optionals, and the Maybe pattern, to manage the absence of values explicitly and avoid unexpected errors.

1. Nullables

In C#, nullable types allow value types (e.g., int, bool) to represent the absence of a value. They are defined using the ? syntax.

Key Features:

Can either hold a value or represent null.
Includes methods like HasValue and GetValueOrDefault() for safe handling.

Example:
csharp
Copy code
int? number = null;

```csharp
if (number.HasValue)
{
    Console.WriteLine($"Value: {number.Value}");
}
else
{
    Console.WriteLine("No value assigned.");
}
```

2. Optionals

Optionals encapsulate a value or its absence, promoting safer and more expressive code. C# doesn't natively have an Optional type, but libraries like LanguageExt or custom implementations provide similar functionality.

Key Features:
Explicitly handles cases of "value" or "no value."
Avoids null references by requiring users to handle both cases.
Example:

csharp
Copy code

```
Option<string> name = Option<string>.None;

name.Match(
    Some: value => Console.WriteLine($"Name:
{value}"),
    None: () => Console.WriteLine("No    name
provided.")
);
```

3. The Maybe Pattern

The Maybe pattern is a functional construct that represents a value or the absence of a value. It's similar to Option or Nullable, but with a strong emphasis on functional handling (e.g., chaining, mapping).

Benefits:
Eliminates null checks.
Encourages chaining operations to process values only when they exist.

Example of Maybe Pattern in C#:

csharp
Copy code

```csharp
public class Maybe<T>
{
    private readonly T? _value;
    public bool HasValue => _value != null;

    private Maybe(T? value) => _value = value;

    public static Maybe<T> Some(T value) =>
new(value);
    public static Maybe<T> None() => new(default);

    public TResult Match<TResult>(Func<T, TResult>
some, Func<TResult> none) =>
        HasValue ? some(_value!) : none();
}

// Usage
var maybeValue = Maybe<int>.Some(10);

int result = maybeValue.Match(
    some: value => value * 2,
    none: () => 0
);
Console.WriteLine(result); // Output: 20
```

Key Differences

Feature	Nullables	Optionals	Maybe Pattern
Native to C#	Yes	No (requires libraries)	No (requires custom implementation)
APPLLIES To	Value types (int?)	Reference & value types	General use
Error handling	Limited (nullable checks)	Explicit handling with Match	Functional chaining & mapping
Functional style	Partial	Yes	Strong functional focus Hi

Advantages

Eliminates NullReferenceException: By replacing nulls with explicit types, these patterns ensure safer code.
Encourages Explicitness: Forces developers to handle "no value" cases explicitly.
Improves Readability: Clearer intent with constructs like Some, None, or Match.

Conclusion

Nullables, optionals, and the Maybe pattern provide robust mechanisms to handle missing values safely and predictably. While nullables are suitable for basic scenarios, optionals and the Maybe pattern offer a more functional and composable approach, aligning well with modern programming practices. Their usage leads to safer, cleaner, and more maintainable code.

10.2 Functional Exception Handling with Result Types

Functional programming promotes predictable and explicit error handling, favoring data-driven constructs over traditional exceptions. One such construct is the Result type, which encapsulates the outcome of an operation, representing either a success or a failure. This approach ensures that errors are handled explicitly, making code more robust and maintainable.

What Are Result Types?

A Result type is a wrapper that holds one of two states:

Success: Contains the result of a successful operation.
Failure: Contains an error message, exception, or failure reason.
Result types avoid implicit control flow disruptions caused by exceptions, enabling functions to return errors as part of their output.

Common Result Type Structure:

```csharp
Copy code
public class Result<T>
{
    public T? Value { get; }
    public string? Error { get; }
    public bool IsSuccess => Error == null;

    private Result(T value) => Value = value;
    private Result(string error) => Error = error;

    public static Result<T> Success(T value) =>
new(value);
    public static Result<T> Failure(string error) =>
new(error);
}
```

Advantages of Result Types

Predictable Behavior: Errors are handled explicitly, making function outcomes easier to anticipate.

Avoids Side Effects: Eliminates exceptions that disrupt control flow.

Composability: Enables chaining operations and propagating errors seamlessly in functional pipelines.

Improved Readability: Encapsulates both success and failure, reducing the need for try-catch blocks.

Using Result Types in C#

Example: Wrapping an Operation

csharp

Copy code

```csharp
public Result<int> Divide(int numerator, int denominator)
{
    if (denominator == 0)
        return Result<int>.Failure("Division by zero is not allowed.");
        return Result<int>.Success(numerator / denominator);
}

// Usage
var result = Divide(10, 0);
if (result.IsSuccess)
    Console.WriteLine($"Result: {result.Value}");
else
    Console.WriteLine($"Error: {result.Error}");
```

Chaining Operations with Result Types

Result types support functional chaining, allowing multiple operations to be composed without manually checking for errors.

Example: Functional Pipeline

csharp
Copy code

```csharp
public Result<int> Parse(string input)
{
    if (int.TryParse(input, out var number))
        return Result<int>.Success(number);
        return Result<int>.Failure("Invalid number format.");
}

public Result<int> AddTen(int number) =>
Result<int>.Success(number + 10);

// Chaining with Result Types
var result = Parse("42")
    .FlatMap(AddTen);

result.Match(
```

```
  success => Console.WriteLine($"Result: {success}"),
  failure => Console.WriteLine($"Error: {failure}")
);
```

Integrating LINQ with Result Types

C# LINQ can be adapted to work with result types, enabling declarative error handling in functional-style queries.

Example:
csharp
Copy code
```
var result = from num in Parse("42")
       from sum in AddTen(num)
       select sum;

result.Match(
  success => Console.WriteLine($"Result: {success}"),
  failure => Console.WriteLine($"Error: {failure}")
);
```

Benefits in Functional Programming

Explicit Error Handling: Avoids hidden errors by treating failures as part of the function's return type.

Simpler Testing: Encapsulated error states are easier to test and mock.

Reduced Runtime Failures: Encourages handling all possible outcomes at compile time.

Challenges

Boilerplate: Result types may require additional code for wrapping and unwrapping values.

Complexity for Newcomers: Developers unfamiliar with functional paradigms might find the approach unintuitive at first.

Conclusion

Functional exception handling with result types offers a safer, clearer, and more predictable alternative to traditional exception handling. By encapsulating both success and failure states, it aligns with functional programming principles, enabling developers to write robust and maintainable code. This approach reduces runtime surprises and ensures that errors are managed explicitly and transparently.

Chapter 11
Asynchronous Functional Programming

Asynchronous functional programming combines functional paradigms with asynchronous workflows, enabling developers to write non-blocking, efficient, and composable code. This approach is particularly useful for applications requiring high concurrency, such as web services, data processing pipelines, and real-time applications.

Core Concepts

Non-Blocking Operations:
Asynchronous functions execute without blocking the main thread, improving performance in I/O-bound or network-intensive tasks.

Composability:

Functional programming enables chaining and combining asynchronous operations through constructs like tasks, promises, or futures.

Immutability:

Data remains immutable, ensuring thread safety and reducing side effects during asynchronous operations.

Declarative Syntax:

Functional programming emphasizes what should be done rather than how, making asynchronous code more readable and maintainable.

Asynchronous Functional Programming in C#

C# provides excellent support for asynchronous functional programming using async/await, LINQ, and functional constructs.

Example: Composing Asynchronous Tasks

```csharp
Copy code
public async Task<string> FetchDataAsync(string url)
{
    using var client = new HttpClient();
    return await client.GetStringAsync(url);
```

```
}

public async Task<int> ProcessDataAsync(string data)
{
    await Task.Delay(100); // Simulating processing
    return data.Length;
}

// Composing Functions
public async Task<int>
GetProcessedDataLengthAsync(string url)
{
    var data = await FetchDataAsync(url);
    return await ProcessDataAsync(data);
}
```

Functional Constructs for Async

LINQ with Async:

LINQ can be adapted for asynchronous pipelines using libraries like System.Linq.Async.

Task Composition:

Functional paradigms like Task.WhenAll and Task.WhenAny allow asynchronous task parallelization and composition.

Error Handling:

Functional error-handling approaches, such as result types, can be extended to asynchronous workflows.

Benefits

Improved Performance: Enables high-concurrency applications with minimal resource consumption.
Composability: Simplifies complex workflows through function chaining.
Maintainability: Declarative and immutable patterns make code cleaner and easier to debug.

Conclusion

Asynchronous functional programming leverages the best of both paradigms, ensuring efficient and expressive solutions for modern software development challenges. By combining immutability, composability, and non-blocking operations, developers can build scalable, maintainable, and robust applications.

11.1 Task and Async/Await in a Functional Context

In modern programming, Task and async/await provide an elegant way to handle asynchronous operations. In a functional programming context, they enable the composition and chaining of asynchronous workflows while adhering to core functional principles like immutability and declarative programming.

Understanding Task and Async/Await

Task: Represents a unit of work that can run asynchronously. It is the backbone of asynchronous programming in C#, providing methods for chaining, combining, and awaiting operations.
async/await: Keywords that simplify working with asynchronous code, making it look like synchronous code while maintaining non-blocking behavior.

Functional Characteristics of Task and Async/Await

Composability:
Tasks can be combined using functional constructs like Task.WhenAll and Task.WhenAny, allowing developers to orchestrate complex workflows.

Declarative Syntax:

The async/await pattern provides a clear and readable way to define the flow of asynchronous operations.

Immutability:
Functional programming discourages mutating shared state during asynchronous operations, promoting thread safety.

Error Propagation:
Tasks naturally propagate exceptions, which can be handled in a functional manner using try/catch or result types like Task<Result<T>>.

Using Task and Async/Await Functionally in C#

Composing Asynchronous Functions

```csharp
Copy code
public async Task<string> GetDataAsync(string url)
{
    using var client = new HttpClient();
    return await client.GetStringAsync(url);
}

public async Task<int> ProcessDataAsync(string data)
{
    await Task.Delay(100); // Simulating processing
    return data.Length;
}

public async Task<int> ExecuteWorkflowAsync(string url)
{
    var data = await GetDataAsync(url);
    return await ProcessDataAsync(data);
}
```

Functional Composition with Task.WhenAll
and Task.WhenAny

Functional programming encourages working with collections of asynchronous tasks.

```csharp
Copy code
public async Task<int[]> ProcessUrlsAsync(string[] urls)
{
        var tasks = urls.Select(async url => await GetDataAsync(url).ContinueWith(task => task.Result.Length));
    return await Task.WhenAll(tasks);
}
```

Error Handling in Functional Context

Instead of using exceptions directly, functional programming leverages constructs like result types to handle errors explicitly in asynchronous workflows.

Example: Using a Result Type

```csharp
Copy code
public async Task<Result<string>> GetDataSafelyAsync(string url)
```

183

```csharp
{
    try
    {
        var data = await GetDataAsync(url);
        return Result<string>.Success(data);
    }
    catch (Exception ex)
    {
        return Result<string>.Failure(ex.Message);
    }
}

// Composing with Result Type
public async Task<Result<int>>
ExecuteSafeWorkflowAsync(string url)
{
    var result = await GetDataSafelyAsync(url);
    return result.IsSuccess
        ? Result<int>.Success(result.Value.Length)
        : Result<int>.Failure(result.Error);
}
```

Advantages in a Functional Context

Improved Code Readability: async/await syntax mirrors synchronous code, making functional operations intuitive.

Chaining and Composability: Tasks allow seamless chaining of asynchronous operations without deep nesting.

Thread Safety: Functional immutability ensures asynchronous workflows avoid shared state issues.

Error Management: Combining tasks with result types simplifies error handling and improves robustness.

Conclusion

Using Task and async/await in a functional context enhances code clarity, composability, and maintainability. By adhering to functional principles like immutability, declarative programming, and explicit error handling, developers can build efficient and reliable asynchronous systems. This approach is particularly beneficial for high-concurrency applications that demand both performance and readability.

11.2 Combining Async Programming with Functional Concepts

Modern software often requires handling asynchronous tasks efficiently. Combining async programming with functional programming concepts allows developers to write scalable, readable, and maintainable code by leveraging immutability, composability, and declarative programming.

Core Functional Concepts in Async Programming

Immutability:

Functional programming promotes immutability, ensuring that asynchronous tasks do not modify shared state, which enhances thread safety.

Composability:

Functions can be composed to build complex asynchronous workflows using constructs like Task.WhenAll and LINQ.

Pure Functions:

Async functions should aim to be pure, returning predictable results based on input without side effects.

Declarative Programming:

Async workflows can be expressed declaratively, focusing on what needs to be done rather than how.

Practical Techniques for Combining Async and Functional Programming

1. Function Composition with Async

Compose multiple asynchronous functions into a pipeline, avoiding deeply nested callbacks.

```csharp
Copy code
public async Task<string> FetchDataAsync(string url)
{
    using var client = new HttpClient();
    return await client.GetStringAsync(url);
}

public async Task<int> CountWordsAsync(string data)
```

```csharp
{
    await Task.Delay(100); // Simulate processing delay
    return data.Split(' ').Length;
}

public async Task<int> ProcessDataAsync(string url)
{
    var data = await FetchDataAsync(url);
    return await CountWordsAsync(data);
}
```

2. Parallel Execution with Tasks

Run multiple asynchronous operations in parallel using Task.WhenAll.

csharp
Copy code
```csharp
public async Task<int[]> ProcessUrlsAsync(string[] urls)
{
    var tasks = urls.Select(url => FetchDataAsync(url).ContinueWith(task => task.Result.Length));
    return await Task.WhenAll(tasks);
```

}

3. Using LINQ with Async

Combine LINQ's declarative style with asynchronous operations using libraries like System.Linq.Async.

csharp
Copy code

```csharp
public async Task<IEnumerable<int>>
ProcessUrlsWithLinqAsync(IEnumerable<string> urls)
{
    return await urls.ToAsyncEnumerable()
                .SelectAwait(async url => (await
FetchDataAsync(url)).Length)
        .ToListAsync();
}
```

4. Error Handling with Functional Constructs

Instead of relying on traditional exceptions, use functional error-handling constructs like Result types.

csharp
Copy code

```csharp
public          async          Task<Result<string>>
SafeFetchDataAsync(string url)
{
  try
  {
                return   Result<string>.Success(await
FetchDataAsync(url));
  }
  catch (Exception ex)
  {
    return Result<string>.Failure(ex.Message);
  }
}
```

Benefits of Combining Async and Functional Programming

Improved Readability: Declarative workflows make complex async operations easier to understand.

Simpler Error Management: Functional constructs like Result<T> make error propagation explicit and predictable.

Thread Safety: Immutability ensures that concurrent tasks do not corrupt shared state.

Reusable Code: Pure and composable functions encourage code reuse across workflows.

Challenges and Best Practices

State Management: Ensure shared state is immutable or properly synchronized to avoid race conditions.

Chaining Complexity: Avoid deeply nested await calls by breaking workflows into composable functions.

Testing: Pure functions and predictable outputs simplify testing, even for asynchronous operations.

Conclusion

Combining asynchronous programming with functional concepts creates a powerful paradigm for building modern applications. By adhering to principles like immutability, composability, and declarative programming, developers can write robust, maintainable, and efficient code that takes full advantage of asynchronous capabilities.

PART V: FUNCTIONAL PROGRAMMING DESIGN PATTERNS

Chapter 12.
Composition over Inheritance

iComposition over inheritance is a design principle that promotes the use of object composition to achieve code reuse and flexibility instead of relying heavily on class inheritance. This principle is particularly valuable in functional programming and modern software design as it encourages modular and maintainable code.

Key Features of Composition
Reusability:

Behavior is encapsulated in independent, reusable components that can be combined.

Flexibility:

Components can be replaced or modified without affecting unrelated parts of the system, enabling easier adaptability.

Decoupling:

Composition leads to less tightly coupled code compared to inheritance, which often creates rigid hierarchies.

Benefits of Composition Over Inheritance
Avoids Fragile Hierarchies:

Changes in base classes can inadvertently affect derived classes in inheritance. Composition sidesteps this problem.

Encourages Modular Design:
With composition, behaviors are added dynamically, keeping objects simpler and focused on specific responsibilities.

Enhances Testability:
Independent components are easier to test in isolation compared to deeply nested inheritance chains.

Example: Using Composition in C#
Instead of creating a large class hierarchy, delegate behavior to components:

With Inheritance:

```csharp
Copy code
public class Animal
{
    public virtual void Speak() =>
Console.WriteLine("Animal sound");
}

public class Dog : Animal
{
    public override void Speak() =>
Console.WriteLine("Bark");
}
```

With Composition:

```csharp
Copy code
public interface ISoundBehavior
{
    void MakeSound();
}

public class BarkBehavior : ISoundBehavior
{
```

```csharp
    public void MakeSound() =>
Console.WriteLine("Bark");
}

public class Animal
{
    private readonly ISoundBehavior _soundBehavior;

    public Animal(ISoundBehavior soundBehavior) =>
_soundBehavior = soundBehavior;

        public void Speak() =>
_soundBehavior.MakeSound();
}

var dog = new Animal(new BarkBehavior());
dog.Speak(); // Output: Bark
```

Conclusion

By emphasizing composition over inheritance, developers can create systems that are more modular, extensible, and maintainable. This approach reduces the risks associated with rigid class hierarchies and allows for greater adaptability in software design.

12.1 Function Composition in C#

Function composition is a functional programming concept that involves combining two or more functions to create a new function, where the output of one function serves as the input to the next. This approach encourages modular, reusable, and readable code. While C# is primarily an object-oriented language, its support for functional programming features like delegates, lambdas, and LINQ makes it well-suited for function composition.

Key Concepts of Function Composition

Chaining Functions:
Functions are linked together, where the output of one becomes the input of another.

Immutability:

Function composition works best with pure functions that do not mutate their inputs.

Declarative Style:
The flow of data through composed functions is easier to understand compared to imperative programming.

Benefits of Function Composition

Modularity: Break down complex logic into smaller, testable functions.
Reusability: Reuse functions across different workflows.
Readability: Clearly express the flow of data and transformations.

Implementing Function Composition in C#

1. Using Lambdas for Composition
C# allows the composition of functions using lambda expressions.

csharp
Copy code
```csharp
Func<int, int> multiplyByTwo = x => x * 2;
Func<int, int> addThree = x => x + 3;
```

```csharp
Func<int, int> composedFunction = x =>
addThree(multiplyByTwo(x));

int result = composedFunction(5); // Output: 13 (5 * 2
+ 3)
```

2. Creating a Generic Compose Function

Define a utility method to compose any two functions.

```csharp
csharp
Copy code
public static Func<T, TResult> Compose<T,
TIntermediate, TResult>(
    Func<TIntermediate, TResult> f,
    Func<T, TIntermediate> g)
{
    return x => f(g(x));
}

// Usage
var multiplyAndAdd = Compose(addThree,
multiplyByTwo);
```

int result = multiplyAndAdd(5); // Output: 13

3. Chaining Functions with LINQ

LINQ's declarative syntax naturally supports function composition for transforming data.

csharp
Copy code
```
var numbers = new[] { 1, 2, 3, 4 };

var results = numbers
    .Select(multiplyByTwo)
    .Select(addThree);

foreach (var result in results)
{
    Console.WriteLine(result); // Output: 5, 7, 9, 11
}
```


4. Pipelines for Composition

Pipelines enable sequential data transformations using composed functions.

```csharp
Copy code
public static TOutput Pipe<TInput, TOutput>(this TInput input, Func<TInput, TOutput> func)
{
    return func(input);
}

int finalResult = 5
    .Pipe(multiplyByTwo)
    .Pipe(addThree);

Console.WriteLine(finalResult); // Output: 13
```

Real-World Applications of Function Composition in C#

Data Processing Pipelines: Compose functions for data validation, transformation, and aggregation.
Middleware in ASP.NET Core: Compose request/response handlers in the HTTP pipeline.
Query Transformations: Use LINQ with composed functions to process collections or database results.

Conclusion

Function composition in C# enhances code modularity, readability, and maintainability by enabling developers to build complex workflows from small, reusable functions. Leveraging lambdas, LINQ, and utilities like Compose or Pipe empowers developers to adopt functional programming principles within an object-oriented environment.

12.2 Alternatives to Inheritance with Functional Patterns

Inheritance, while a powerful tool in object-oriented programming, often leads to rigid and tightly coupled code. Functional programming offers several alternatives to inheritance, focusing on composability, immutability, and higher-order functions to achieve flexibility and reusability without the complexities of deep class hierarchies.

1. Composition Over Inheritance

Rather than creating rigid inheritance hierarchies, functional patterns favor composition, where objects or functions are combined to build complex behavior.

Example in C#:

```csharp
Copy code
public interface IBehavior
{
    void Execute();
}

public class LogBehavior : IBehavior
{
            public void Execute() => Console.WriteLine("Logging...");
}

public class SaveBehavior : IBehavior
{
            public void Execute() => Console.WriteLine("Saving...");
}
```

```csharp
public class Processor
{
    private readonly IBehavior _behavior;

    public Processor(IBehavior behavior) => _behavior
= behavior;

    public void Process() => _behavior.Execute();
}

var processor = new Processor(new LogBehavior());
processor.Process(); // Output: Logging...
```

Here, behaviors are composed instead of being inherited, allowing flexibility and modularity.

2. Higher-Order Functions

Functions that take other functions as arguments or return functions enable dynamic behavior without inheritance.

Example:
csharp
Copy code

```csharp
Func<int, int> doubleValue = x => x * 2;
Func<int, int> addFive = x => x + 5;

Func<int, int> composedFunction = x =>
addFive(doubleValue(x));

Console.WriteLine(composedFunction(3)); // Output:
11
```

Higher-order functions make it easy to build reusable, composable units of logic.

3. Type Classes and Traits

Functional programming languages often use type classes (similar to interfaces in C#) to define reusable behaviors, avoiding the need for inheritance.

Example:
csharp
Copy code
```csharp
public interface ITransform<T>
{
    T Transform(T input);
}
```

```csharp
public class SquareTransform : ITransform<int>
{
    public int Transform(int input) => input * input;
}

public static void ApplyTransform<T>(T input,
ITransform<T> transformer)
{
    Console.WriteLine(transformer.Transform(input));
}
```

ApplyTransform(5, new SquareTransform()); // Output: 25
This pattern generalizes behavior without requiring inheritance.

4. Pattern Matching and Case Analysis

Pattern matching allows for branching logic based on the type or structure of data, eliminating the need for polymorphic inheritance.

Example:
csharp
Copy code

```csharp
public static string Describe(object obj) => obj switch
{
    int n when n > 0 => "Positive integer",
    int n when n < 0 => "Negative integer",
    string s => "A string: " + s,
    _ => "Unknown type"
};
```

```csharp
Console.WriteLine(Describe(42)); // Output: Positive integer
```

Pattern matching simplifies handling different cases without a complex class hierarchy.

5. Immutability and Algebraic Data Types

Functional patterns often replace inheritance with algebraic data types (ADTs), where data is immutable and structured into simple, composable types.

Example:

```csharp
csharp
Copy code
public record Shape;
```

```csharp
public record Circle(double Radius) : Shape;
public record Rectangle(double Width, double Height) : Shape;

public static double CalculateArea(Shape shape) =>
shape switch
{
    Circle c => Math.PI * c.Radius * c.Radius,
    Rectangle r => r.Width * r.Height,
    _ => 0
};

Console.WriteLine(CalculateArea(new Circle(5))); // Output: 78.54
```

ADTs enable a functional approach to polymorphism without inheritance.

6. Dependency Injection and Strategy Pattern

In functional programming, behaviors can be injected as dependencies or passed as higher-order functions to achieve dynamic behavior.

Example with Delegates:
csharp

```
Copy code
public class Worker
{
    private readonly Action _work;  in

    public Worker(Action work) => _work = work;

    public void DoWork() => _work();
}

var worker = new Worker(() =>
Console.WriteLine("Working..."));
worker.DoWork(); // Output: Working...
```

This approach decouples behavior from the class definition.

7. Pipelines and Middleware

Functional patterns often use pipelines to process data or execute behavior in stages, avoiding inheritance-based chains.

Example:

csharp

```
Copy code
public static T Pipe<T>(T input, params Func<T, T>[]
functions)
{
    return functions.Aggregate(input, (current, func)
=> func(current));
}


var result = Pipe(5, x => x * 2, x => x + 3);
Console.WriteLine(result); // Output: 13
```

Advantages of Functional Alternatives

Flexibility: Avoids rigid class hierarchies, enabling easier code refactoring.

Reusability: Modular functions and components are easy to reuse across applications.

Testability: Pure functions and independent components are simpler to test in isolation.

Readability: Declarative patterns like pipelines and pattern matching make code easier to follow.

Conclusion

Functional programming offers powerful alternatives to inheritance by emphasizing composition, higher-order functions, pattern matching, and immutability. These patterns encourage clean, modular, and maintainable code while avoiding the pitfalls of rigid inheritance hierarchies. In C#, combining functional patterns with object-oriented techniques provides a balanced approach to building robust software systems.

Chapter 13
Currying and Partial Application

Currying and partial application are foundational concepts in functional programming that allow functions to be more flexible and reusable by transforming how arguments are supplied.

Currying
Currying is the process of transforming a function that takes multiple arguments into a series of functions, each taking a single argument.

Example in C#:

```csharp
Copy code
Func<int, Func<int, int>> curriedAdd = x => y => x + y;

var addFive = curriedAdd(5);
Console.WriteLine(addFive(3)); // Output: 8
```

Here, curriedAdd first takes x and returns a function that takes y, allowing arguments to be supplied one at a time.

Partial Application

Partial application is the process of fixing some arguments of a function and producing another function with fewer arguments.

Example in C#:

csharp

Copy code

```csharp
Func<int, int, int> add = (x, y) => x + y;

Func<int, int> addFive = y => add(5, y);
Console.WriteLine(addFive(3)); // Output: 8
```

Here, addFive partially applies the add function by fixing the first argument to 5.

Key Differences

Currying splits a function into nested functions, each taking one argument.

Partial Application fixes specific arguments of a function, reducing the number of arguments needed for subsequent calls.

Advantages in Functional Programming

Reusability: Makes functions more modular and easier to reuse.
Code Clarity: Simplifies the function signature for specific use cases.
Composability: Facilitates combining smaller functions into larger operations.

By leveraging currying and partial application, C# developers can write more expressive and reusable functional code.

13.1 Implementing Currying in C#

Currying is the process of breaking down a function that takes multiple arguments into a series of functions, each taking a single argument. This functional programming technique is not natively supported in C#, but it can be implemented using higher-order functions and lambdas.

Why Use Currying in C#?

Modularity: Break complex logic into smaller, composable units.
Reusability: Enable partial application of arguments for specific use cases.
Flexibility: Create functions dynamically by progressively applying arguments.

Basic Implementation of Currying

A simple example of currying with a function that adds two numbers:

csharp
Copy code
```csharp
Func<int, Func<int, int>> curriedAdd = x => y => x + y;

// Using the curried function:
var addFive = curriedAdd(5);
```

Console.WriteLine(addFive(3)); // Output: 8

In this example, curriedAdd takes one argument (x) and returns another function that takes the second argument (y) and computes the sum.

Generalized Currying Implementation

To curry a function with any number of arguments, you can create a utility method:

Utility for Currying:

csharp
Copy code
```csharp
public static Func<T1, Func<T2, TResult>> Curry<T1, T2, TResult>(Func<T1, T2, TResult> func)
{
    return x => y => func(x, y);
}
```

Usage:

csharp

Copy code

```
Func<int, int, int> add = (x, y) => x + y;
var curriedAdd = Curry(add);

var addTen = curriedAdd(10);
Console.WriteLine(addTen(5)); // Output: 15
```

This utility method transforms a two-argument function into a curried version that can be progressively called.

Currying for Functions with More Than Two Arguments
You can extend currying to functions with more arguments by nesting further:

Utility for Multi-Argument Currying:

csharp
Copy code

```
public static Func<T1, Func<T2, Func<T3,
TResult>>> Curry<T1, T2, T3, TResult>(Func<T1,
T2, T3, TResult> func)
{
    return x => y => z => func(x, y, z);
}
```
Usage:

csharp
Copy code

```csharp
Func<int, int, int, int> multiply = (x, y, z) => x * y * z;
var curriedMultiply = Curry(multiply);

var multiplyByTwo = curriedMultiply(2);
var multiplyByTwoAndThree = multiplyByTwo(3);
Console.WriteLine(multiplyByTwoAndThree(4));    // Output: 24
```

Practical Use Cases for Currying in C#

Configuration Functions: Define default parameters and reuse functions with specific configurations.

Event Handling: Partially apply handlers for dynamic arguments.

Data Transformation Pipelines: Build modular pipelines with currying for transformations.

Advantages of Implementing Currying

Improved Readability: Cleaner, more expressive function calls.

Reusability: Functions can be applied to different contexts without rewriting.

Composability: Currying simplifies building higher-order functions.

Conclusion

Although currying is not a built-in feature in C#, it can be implemented using lambdas and higher-order functions. By applying currying, developers can write modular, reusable, and composable code, enabling functional programming practices within C#.

13.2 Real-World Applications of Partial Functions

Partial functions, also known as partially applied functions, are a powerful functional programming concept where a function is created by fixing some of its arguments while leaving others to be supplied later. In C#, partial functions enable modular, reusable, and flexible code. Here are some real-world applications of partial functions:

1. Configuring Functions for Specific Scenarios

Partial functions allow developers to configure a general-purpose function for a specific use case by fixing certain arguments.

Example: Logging with a Fixed Log Level

csharp

Copy code

```csharp
Func<string, string, string> log = (level, message) => $"[{level}] {message}";

var infoLogger = (string message) => log("INFO", message);
var errorLogger = (string message) => log("ERROR", message);

Console.WriteLine(infoLogger("System started.")); // Output: [INFO] System started.
Console.WriteLine(errorLogger("System failure.")); // Output: [ERROR] System failure.
```

This approach simplifies log handling by creating specialized loggers for different severity levels.

2. Building Reusable UI Components

In modern UI frameworks, partial functions can help configure components dynamically.

Example: Partial Application for Button Click Handlers

```csharp
Copy code
Func<string, Action> createClickHandler = (buttonName) =>
    () => Console.WriteLine($"{buttonName} clicked");

var saveHandler = createClickHandler("Save");
var cancelHandler = createClickHandler("Cancel");

saveHandler();   // Output: Save clicked
cancelHandler(); // Output: Cancel clicked
```

Here, a general createClickHandler function is customized for specific buttons.

3. API Client Wrappers

Partial functions can simplify API calls by fixing common parameters such as authentication tokens or base URLs.

Example: API Client Setup

```csharp
Copy code
Func<string, string, string, string> apiCall = (baseUrl, token, endpoint) =>
    $"Calling {baseUrl}/{endpoint} with token {token}";

var clientWithToken = (string endpoint) => apiCall("https://api.example.com", "my-token", endpoint);

Console.WriteLine(clientWithToken("users"));    // Output: Calling https://api.example.com/users with token my-token
```

This eliminates the need to repeatedly specify the base URL and token.

4. Enhancing Data Processing Pipelines

In data transformation workflows, partial functions can help streamline repetitive operations.

Example: Data Normalization

csharp
Copy code
```
Func<double, double, double, double> normalize = (min, max, value) => (value - min) / (max - min);

var normalizeTemperature = (double temp) => normalize(-30, 50, temp);

Console.WriteLine(normalizeTemperature(20));      // Output: 0.625
```

By fixing the range parameters, the function is specialized for temperature normalization.

5. Optimizing Mathematical Calculations

Partial functions simplify mathematical modeling by fixing constants or coefficients.

Example: Creating Quadratic Equations

csharp
Copy code

```csharp
Func<double, double, double, double> quadratic = (a, b, c) => (x) => a * x * x + b * x + c;

var simpleQuadratic = quadratic(1, 0, 0); // y = x^2
Console.WriteLine(simpleQuadratic(3));   // Output: 9
```

This approach allows creating reusable equations with fixed coefficients.

6. Dynamic Middleware and Filters

Partial functions can be used to create dynamic middleware for filtering or transforming data streams.

Example: Middleware for Filtering Strings

csharp
Copy code

```csharp
Func<string, bool> filter = (substring) => (input) => input.Contains(substring);
```

```csharp
var errorFilter = filter("Error");
Console.WriteLine(errorFilter("Error:    File    not found")); // Output: True
```

This helps build flexible and reusable data processing pipelines.

7. Event Subscription in Real-Time Systems

Partial functions allow dynamic subscription to events by partially applying the event source or parameters.

Example: Event Listeners

csharp

Copy code

```csharp
Func<string, string, Action> subscribe = (eventSource, eventType) =>
    () => Console.WriteLine($"Listening to {eventType} on {eventSource}");

var systemEvents = subscribe("System", "Startup");
systemEvents(); // Output: Listening to Startup on System
```

This approach simplifies event handling and reduces boilerplate code.

Benefits of Using Partial Functions in Real-World Applications

Code Reusability: Reduces redundancy by reusing generalized functions with fixed arguments.

Simplified API: Creates specialized interfaces for complex operations.

Readability: Improves code clarity by narrowing function focus.

Composability: Facilitates integration with other functional patterns like function composition.

Conclusion

Partial functions are a versatile tool for handling repetitive logic, creating reusable configurations, and streamlining data processing in real-world C# applications. By strategically applying this concept, developers can build cleaner, more maintainable, and highly flexible code.

Chapter 14
Reactive Extensions (Rx) in C#

Reactive Extensions (Rx) is a library for composing asynchronous and event-based programs using observable sequences. It allows developers to handle data streams and events in a functional, declarative way, making it ideal for scenarios involving asynchronous operations, real-time data, or complex event processing.

Core Concepts

Observable: Represents a data stream that can emit values over time.
Observer: Consumes the data emitted by an observable.
Subscription: Links an observer to an observable.
Operators: Provide methods to transform, filter, and combine observable sequences.

Key Features

Asynchronous Data Streams: Rx enables handling streams of data or events asynchronously, such as UI events, API responses, or file updates.
Functional Composition: Operators like Select, Where, and Merge allow you to manipulate data streams concisely.
Error Handling: Built-in mechanisms for managing errors in asynchronous flows.

Example: Observing a Timer

```csharp
Copy code
using System;
using System.Reactive.Linq;

var observable = Observable.Interval(TimeSpan.FromSeconds(1));
var subscription = observable.Subscribe(value => Console.WriteLine($"Tick: {value}"));

Console.ReadLine(); // Keeps the program running to observe ticks
```

In this example, the observable emits a tick every second, and the observer reacts by printing it to the console.

Common Use Cases

UI Event Handling: React to user interactions in a declarative manner.
Real-Time Data Processing: Handle streams of live data, such as stock prices or sensor readings.
Asynchronous APIs: Simplify working with APIs by chaining transformations and reactions.
Error Recovery: Manage retries and fallback logic gracefully.

Advantages

Declarative Code: Simplifies complex asynchronous workflows.
Composability: Enables chaining and combining multiple data streams.
Thread Safety: Provides mechanisms for safely handling concurrency.

Rx in C# is a powerful tool for building responsive, scalable, and maintainable applications in scenarios requiring robust event and data stream handling.

14.1 Introduction to Rx and Observables

Reactive Extensions (Rx) is a programming library designed to simplify working with asynchronous and event-driven programming. It builds on the observer pattern and functional programming concepts to enable efficient handling of streams of data or events. The core building block of Rx is the observable.

What Are Observables?

An observable is a data source that emits a sequence of values over time. These values can be anything: numbers, objects, events, or even errors. Observables enable developers to represent asynchronous operations (like API calls or UI events) as composable sequences of data.

Key Characteristics:

Asynchronous: Observables handle data emission asynchronously.
Push-based: Observables "push" data to subscribers (observers).

Composable: Observables can be transformed, combined, and filtered using operators.

How Observables Work

The observable pattern involves three main players:

Observable: The source of data or events.
Observer: The entity that subscribes to the observable to receive notifications.
Subscription: The link between an observable and an observer.

Lifecycle:
OnNext: Emits a value to the observer.
OnError: Sends an error notification if something goes wrong.
OnCompleted: Signals the end of the data stream.

Basic Observable Example

csharp

Copy code
using System;

```
using System.Reactive.Linq;

var observable = Observable.Range(1, 5); // Emits
numbers 1 through 5
observable.Subscribe(
   value => Console.WriteLine($"Received: {value}"), //
OnNext
            error => Console.WriteLine($"Error:
{error.Message}"), // OnError
         () => Console.WriteLine("Completed!") //
OnCompleted
);
```

Output:

```makefile
Copy code
Received: 1
Received: 2
Received: 3
Received: 4
Received: 5
Completed!
```

Advantages of Rx and Observables

Unified Model: Handles events, asynchronous data, and error handling uniformly.

Functional Approach: Enables transformations and filtering using operators like Select, Where, and GroupBy.

Simplifies Concurrency: Built-in support for thread safety and scheduling.

Declarative Style: Simplifies expressing complex workflows.

Applications of Rx and Observables

User Interface: React to button clicks, input changes, or animations.

Real-Time Systems: Process streams of live data, such as stock prices or GPS coordinates.

Error Recovery: Retry or fallback on failure scenarios in API calls or file operations.

Data Pipelines: Build robust ETL (Extract, Transform, Load) workflows.

Conclusion

Rx and observables revolutionize the way developers approach asynchronous and event-driven programming. By leveraging declarative code, composability, and built-in support for error handling, Rx makes complex workflows manageable and enhances code readability and maintainability.

14.2 Functional Reactive Programming with Rx.NET

Functional Reactive Programming (FRP) is a paradigm that combines functional programming principles with reactive programming to handle asynchronous data streams and events in a declarative, efficient manner. Rx.NET, the .NET implementation of Reactive Extensions, is a powerful library for implementing FRP in .NET applications.

Core Concepts of FRP in Rx.NET

Streams as First-Class Citizens:

In FRP, data streams (events or asynchronous operations) are treated as first-class entities. Rx.NET represents these streams using observables.

Immutability:

Functional programming emphasizes immutability, ensuring that data transformations do not modify the original data but instead produce new values.

Composability:

Rx.NET allows combining, filtering, and transforming streams using declarative operators like Select, Where, Merge, and CombineLatest.

Declarative Code:
Developers specify what should happen to data streams, rather than how to handle them. This leads to cleaner and more maintainable code.

Key Features of Rx.NET for FRP

Observable Sequences:

Rx.NET provides the IObservable<T> interface to represent asynchronous data streams. These streams can emit data, errors, or completion notifications.

Functional Operators:

Rx.NET includes a rich set of operators to process streams, such as:

Transform: Select, SelectMany.
Filter: Where, TakeWhile.
Combine: Merge, Zip, CombineLatest.
Error Handling:
Operators like Catch and Retry handle errors gracefully without disrupting the flow of data.

Schedulers:

Rx.NET provides control over concurrency using schedulers, allowing seamless management of thread pools, UI threads, and more.

Example: Functional Data Transformation with Rx.NET

csharp

```
Copy code
using System;
using System.Reactive.Linq;

class Program
{
    static void Main()
    {
        var observable = Observable.Range(1, 10)
            .Where(x => x % 2 == 0) // Filter: Even numbers
              .Select(x => x * x);   // Transform: Square each
number

        observable.Subscribe(
            value => Console.WriteLine($"Value: {value}"),
                    error => Console.WriteLine($"Error:
{error.Message}"),
            () => Console.WriteLine("Completed!")
        );
    }
}
```

Output:

makefile
Copy code

Value: 4
Value: 16
Value: 36
Value: 64
Value: 100
Completed!

Advantages of FRP with Rx.NET

Declarative Asynchronous Code:
Simplifies managing complex asynchronous workflows by focusing on what to do, not how.

Event Streams Simplified:

Efficiently handle streams of events or data with clean, functional operators.

Error Resilience:

Streamlined mechanisms for error handling and recovery, ensuring robust applications.

Concurrency Made Easy:

Built-in support for concurrent stream processing through schedulers.

Applications of Rx.NET in FRP

Real-Time Applications:

Live data feeds (e.g., stock market prices).
Real-time sensor data processing.

User Interfaces:

Reacting to user interactions (button clicks, text input).

Animation sequencing.

Data Pipelines:

ETL workflows with complex transformations.
Asynchronous APIs:

Handling retries, timeouts, and fallbacks with ease.

Conclusion

Functional Reactive Programming with Rx.NET empowers developers to build robust, maintainable, and responsive systems. By integrating functional principles with reactive programming, Rx.NET simplifies the management of asynchronous data and event streams, ensuring efficient, declarative, and error-tolerant solutions for modern applications.

PART VI: CASE STUDIES AND PRACTICAL EXAMPLES

Chapter 15
Building a Functional C# Application

Creating a functional C# application involves leveraging functional programming principles to design clean, maintainable, and efficient systems. The goal is to minimize side effects, use immutable data structures, and rely on declarative programming techniques.

Key Principles

Immutability:

Use immutable objects to prevent unintended state changes, ensuring safer and more predictable code.

csharp
Copy code

record Person(string Name, int Age); // Immutable data structure

Pure Functions:

Write functions that depend only on their inputs and return outputs without modifying external state.

```csharp
Copy code
int Add(int a, int b) => a + b; // Pure function
```

Higher-Order Functions:

Use functions as first-class citizens to enhance code reuse and composability.

```csharp
Copy code
Func<int, int> Square = x => x * x;
```

Declarative Style:

Use LINQ and other functional patterns to express what to do rather than how.

csharp

Copy code

```csharp
var evens = numbers.Where(x => x % 2 == 0).Select(x => x * x);
```

Steps to Build a Functional C# Application

Define Immutable Data Models:
Use record types or immutable collections for safer state management.

Write Pure Functions:
Break down the application into smaller, reusable, and testable functions.

Leverage LINQ:

Use LINQ for data transformations and filtering, ensuring a declarative approach to collection processing.

Handle Errors Functionally:

Implement error handling patterns like Result<T> or the Maybe monad to manage failures gracefully.

Use Rx.NET for Reactive Patterns:

Handle asynchronous streams and events with observables, enabling a responsive application design.

Example: A Simple Functional Pipeline

csharp
Copy code
```csharp
var numbers = new[] { 1, 2, 3, 4, 5 };
var result = numbers
    .Where(x => x % 2 == 0)   // Filter even numbers
    .Select(x => x * x)       // Square each number
    .ToList();

result.ForEach(Console.WriteLine);
```
Output:

Copy code
```
4
16
```

Benefits

Readability: Declarative code is easier to understand.

Maintainability: Smaller, pure functions are simpler to test and debug.

Scalability: Immutability and functional patterns enable concurrent and parallel programming.

Functional programming in C# provides a robust foundation for building reliable, scalable applications with clean and concise code.

15.1 End-to-End Functional Application Design

Building an end-to-end functional application in C# involves applying functional programming principles at every stage of the development process. This approach results in modular, maintainable, and testable software systems that minimize side effects and improve reliability.

Key Components of Functional Application Design

Domain Modeling with Immutability:

Use immutable data structures (record types) to model the domain.
Ensure that data remains consistent and free from unintended modifications.

Example:
csharp
Copy code
public record Product(string Name, decimal Price);

Functional Data Flow:

Data transformations and operations are performed using pure functions.

Use pipelines and higher-order functions for processing.
Example:
csharp
Copy code
```
var products = new List<Product>
{
    new("Laptop", 1000m),
    new("Mouse", 50m),
```

```csharp
};
```

```csharp
var discountedProducts = products
    .Where(p => p.Price > 100)
    .Select(p => new Product(p.Name, p.Price * 0.9m))
    .ToList();
```

Declarative Logic with LINQ:

Use LINQ for querying and transforming collections or databases.
It simplifies code and makes the intent clear.

Error Handling:

Use functional patterns like Result<T> or Option<T> to handle errors gracefully without relying on exceptions.

Example:

csharp
Copy code

```
public  Result<decimal>  Divide(decimal  numerator,
decimal denominator) =>
    denominator == 0
        ? Result.Fail<decimal>("Cannot divide by zero")
        : Result.Ok(numerator / denominator);
```

Reactive Programming:

Use Rx.NET for handling asynchronous streams of data, such as UI events or real-time updates.
Observables make it easier to manage concurrency and event-driven logic.

Composability and Modularity:

Break the application into smaller, reusable modules.
Functions are composed to build complex workflows without duplication.

Design Process for a Functional Application

Requirements Gathering and Domain Definition:

Identify the key entities and their relationships in the domain.

Define the behavior as pure functions that operate on these entities.

Application Layers:

Data Layer: Use immutable data structures and functional collections.
Business Logic Layer: Implement pure functions for core logic.
Presentation Layer: React to events using functional reactive programming (e.g., Rx.NET).

Pipeline-Driven Workflow:

Design data flow pipelines to transform input into output in a series of pure, composable steps.

Error and State Management:

Implement a central functional error-handling strategy.
Use immutability to manage state transitions effectively.

Example of End-to-End Workflow

Problem: Create an e-commerce system that applies discounts to products based on user input.

csharp

Copy code

```csharp
// Step 1: Define Immutable Data Model
public record Product(string Name, decimal Price);

// Step 2: Pure Function for Discount Calculation
Func<Product, decimal, Product> applyDiscount =
(product, discount) =>
   new(product.Name, product.Price * (1 - discount));

// Step 3: Declarative Pipeline
var products = new List<Product>
{
   new("Laptop", 1000m),
   new("Mouse", 50m),
   new("Keyboard", 150m),
};

decimal discount = 0.10m;

var discountedProducts = products
   .Where(p => p.Price > 100)        // Filter
```

```
    .Select(p => applyDiscount(p, discount))    //
Transform
    .ToList();

// Step 4: Display Results
discountedProducts.ForEach(p                     =>
Console.WriteLine($"{p.Name}: {p.Price:C}"));
```

Advantages of End-to-End Functional Design

Clarity and Simplicity: Code is easier to understand and
modify.
Error Resilience: Functional patterns ensure consistent error
handling.
Testability: Pure functions are straightforward to test.
Concurrency-Friendly: Immutability and composability
simplify parallelism.
Scalability: Declarative pipelines handle growth in
complexity seamlessly.

Conclusion

End-to-end functional application design in C# allows developers to build scalable, reliable, and maintainable systems. By adhering to functional principles like immutability, pure functions, and composability, developers can create software that is robust, concise, and adaptable to change.

15.2 Combining Functional and Object-Oriented Approaches

C# is a multiparadigm language, allowing developers to blend functional programming (FP) and object-oriented programming (OOP) to create robust, maintainable, and efficient applications. By combining the strengths of both paradigms, developers can achieve code that is modular, testable, and scalable.

Key Concepts of the Hybrid Approach

Encapsulation of State (OOP):

Use classes and objects to encapsulate data and manage state. Functional methods can operate on immutable objects to minimize side effects.

Behavior with Pure Functions (FP):

Write stateless, pure functions for logic and transformations.
Pure functions ensure code reliability and testability.

Immutability:

Combine immutable data structures (FP) with encapsulated behavior (OOP).
Use record types or readonly fields in classes for immutability.

Higher-Order Functions with Object Methods:

Pass methods as delegates or lambda expressions to other methods or classes.
Enhance reusability and abstraction.

Benefits of Combining FP and OOP

Code Reusability:

Use inheritance and interfaces (OOP) alongside composable functional pipelines (FP).

Maintainability:

Encapsulation simplifies the management of complex state, while pure functions reduce unexpected side effects.
Flexibility:

OOP handles complex domains with encapsulation, while FP simplifies logic with declarative constructs.
Concurrency:

Immutability (FP) combined with state encapsulation (OOP) makes concurrent programming safer and more intuitive.

Designing a Hybrid System

Example: A Banking Application

Domain Model (OOP):

Use classes to represent entities like Account.

csharp
Copy code

```csharp
public class Account
{
    public string Id { get; }
    public decimal Balance { get; private set; }

    public Account(string id, decimal balance)
    {
        Id = id;
        Balance = balance;
    }

    public void Deposit(decimal amount)
    {
        Balance += amount;
    }
}
```

Business Logic (FP):

Use pure functions for business rules like transaction validation.

csharp
Copy code

```csharp
public static bool IsValidTransaction(decimal amount)
=> amount > 0;
```

Declarative Workflow (FP):

Combine LINQ and functional pipelines to process data.

csharp
Copy code
```csharp
var transactions = new[] { 100m, -50m, 200m, -150m };
var validTransactions = transactions.Where(IsValidTransaction).Sum();
```

Combining Functionality (Hybrid):

Encapsulate state changes while leveraging functional pipelines.

csharp
Copy code
```csharp
Account account = new Account("12345", 1000m);

transactions
  .Where(IsValidTransaction)
```

```
.ToList()
.ForEach(account.Deposit);

Console.WriteLine($"New                    Balance:
{account.Balance}");
```

Challenges and Solutions

State Management:

Challenge: OOP encourages mutable state, while FP avoids it.
Solution: Use immutability wherever possible and encapsulate state transitions within objects.

Complexity:

Challenge: Mixing paradigms can add complexity.

Solution: Clearly separate functional logic from object-oriented components.

Interoperability:

Challenge: Combining pure functions with classes may feel disjointed.

Solution: Use dependency injection to manage functional services in OOP systems.

Conclusion

Combining functional and object-oriented programming in C# leverages the best of both paradigms. By encapsulating state with OOP and implementing logic using functional principles, developers can create applications that are both flexible and maintainable. This hybrid approach is particularly powerful for modern software development, where scalability, reliability, and simplicity are critical.

Chapter 16
Real-World Examples

Combining functional and object-oriented paradigms in C# allows developers to design versatile applications for various real-world scenarios. Here are some examples:

1. Web API Development
OOP Usage: Define controllers, services, and models to handle HTTP requests and encapsulate application logic.
FP Usage: Use LINQ for filtering, mapping, and transforming data, and implement pure functions for business rules.

Example:

A user service encapsulates the state, while functional logic validates user input and applies transformations:

```csharp
Copy code
public class UserService
{
    private readonly List<User> _users;
```

```csharp
public UserService() => _users = new List<User>();

public IEnumerable<User> GetActiveUsers() =>
    _users.Where(user => user.IsActive).ToList();
}
```

2. Data Processing Pipelines

OOP Usage: Encapsulate configuration and execution context in classes.
FP Usage: Use functional pipelines to process large datasets.

Example:
A financial application processes transactions using LINQ:
csharp
Copy code
```csharp
var transactions = new List<Transaction>
{
    new("Deposit", 1000m),
    new("Withdrawal", -200m)
};

var total = transactions
    .Where(t => t.Amount > 0)
    .Sum(t => t.Amount);
```

3. Reactive Applications

OOP Usage: Create objects to represent UI components and manage state.
FP Usage: Use Rx.NET to handle asynchronous data streams and events.

Example:

In a chat application, observables manage real-time message streams:

csharp
Copy code

```csharp
var messages = new Subject<string>();

messages
   .Where(msg => !string.IsNullOrEmpty(msg))
   .Subscribe(Console.WriteLine);

messages.OnNext("Hello, World!");
```

4. Immutable Configuration Management

OOP Usage: Represent configuration as objects.

FP Usage: Use immutable records and pure functions to handle configuration transformations.

Example:
csharp
Copy code
```csharp
public record AppConfig(string Name, string Version);

var config = new AppConfig("MyApp", "1.0");
var updatedConfig = config with { Version = "1.1" };
```

5. Gaming Engines

OOP Usage: Use classes to represent game entities, such as characters and objects.
FP Usage: Implement pure functions for calculations like physics or AI decisions.

Example:
csharp
Copy code
```csharp
public class Character
{
    public string Name { get; set; }
```

```csharp
    public int Health { get; private set; }

    public void ApplyDamage(int damage) => Health -=
damage;
}
```

```csharp
Func<int, int, int> calculateDamage = (baseDamage,
multiplier) => baseDamage * multiplier;
```

Conclusion

These real-world examples demonstrate how blending object-oriented and functional paradigms in C# enhances application scalability, reliability, and maintainability while leveraging the strengths of both approaches.

16.1 Refactoring Imperative Code to Functional Code

Refactoring imperative code into functional code involves transforming a step-by-step, state-driven approach into a declarative, immutable, and pure-function-oriented style. This process enhances code readability, testability, and maintainability by reducing side effects and emphasizing function composition.

Key Strategies for Refactoring

Eliminate Mutable State

Imperative Style: Uses variables to track changing state.
Functional Style: Replaces mutable state with immutable variables.

Example:
```csharp
Copy code
// Imperative
int sum = 0;
foreach (var num in numbers)
{
    sum += num;
}

// Functional
var sum = numbers.Sum();
```

Replace Loops with Higher-Order Functions

Imperative Style: Explicit loops for iteration.

Functional Style: Use LINQ or higher-order functions like Select, Where, and Aggregate.

Example:

```csharp
Copy code
// Imperative
var evens = new List<int>();
foreach (var num in numbers)
{
    if (num % 2 == 0) evens.Add(num);
}

// Functional
var evens = numbers.Where(num => num % 2 == 0).ToList();
```

Adopt Pure Functions

Imperative Style: Functions with side effects or dependencies on global state.

Functional Style: Functions that return the same output for the same input.

Example:
csharp
Copy code
// Imperative
public int Increment(ref int value) => ++value;

// Functional
public int Increment(int value) => value + 1;

Replace Conditionals with Pattern Matching

Imperative Style: Uses nested if-else statements.

Functional Style: Leverages pattern matching for more concise and expressive logic.
Example:
csharp
Copy code
// Imperative
string GetStatus(int score)
{
   if (score < 50) return "Fail";

```csharp
    else if (score < 75) return "Pass";
    return "Excellent";
}

// Functional
string GetStatus(int score) => score switch
{
    < 50 => "Fail",
    < 75 => "Pass",
    _ => "Excellent"
};
```

Use Function Composition

Imperative Style: Breaks tasks into multiple steps.
Functional Style: Combines functions to create pipelines.

Example:

csharp
Copy code
```csharp
// Imperative
var filtered = numbers.Where(num => num % 2 == 0);
var doubled = filtered.Select(num => num * 2);

// Functional
```

```csharp
var result = numbers.Where(num => num % 2 == 0).Select(num => num * 2);
```

Benefits of Refactoring to Functional Code

Improved Readability: Declarative style allows developers to understand "what" is being done rather than "how."

Ease of Testing: Pure functions are easier to test due to the absence of side effects.

Enhanced Parallelism: Immutability and stateless computations enable safer concurrent execution.

Reduced Bugs: Immutable data structures and pure functions minimize unintended behavior.

Refactoring Example: A Complex Scenario

Imperative Code

```csharp
Copy code
public int CalculateTotalDiscount(List<Order> orders)
{
    int totalDiscount = 0;
    foreach (var order in orders)
    {
```

```csharp
    if (order.Amount > 100)
    {
        totalDiscount += 10;
    }
    else
    {
        totalDiscount += 5;
    }
  }
  return totalDiscount;
}
```

Functional Refactor

csharp
Copy code
```csharp
public int CalculateTotalDiscount(List<Order> orders)
=>
    orders.Sum(order => order.Amount > 100 ? 10 : 5);
```

Challenges in Refactoring

Transitioning Large Codebases: Incremental refactoring is essential to avoid breaking existing functionality.

Performance Considerations: Certain functional constructs may introduce overhead; careful optimization is necessary. Learning Curve: Teams need to be familiar with functional programming principles and idioms.

Conclusion

Refactoring imperative code into functional code in C# can significantly enhance maintainability, scalability, and correctness. By leveraging functional programming principles like immutability, higher-order functions, and pure functions, developers can write cleaner, more reliable code while preserving the flexibility of the C# language.

16.2 Performance and Maintainability Comparisons

Functional programming (FP) and imperative programming (IP) represent two distinct paradigms, each with strengths and trade-offs. Comparing their performance and maintainability provides insights into choosing the best approach based on application requirements.

Performance Comparisons

Execution Speed

Imperative Programming:

Typically faster in raw performance due to its reliance on mutable state and direct manipulation of memory.
Often optimized by compilers for procedural tasks.

Example: For-loops in IP tend to outperform higher-order functions like LINQ in scenarios involving a high volume of data.

Functional Programming:

May incur overhead from immutability and function calls.
Recursion (often used in FP) can be less efficient than iterative loops unless optimized with techniques like tail-call optimization.

Memory Usage

Imperative Programming:

Efficient due to in-place updates and mutable data structures.

However, shared mutable state can lead to memory corruption in concurrent applications.

Functional Programming:

Uses immutable data structures, which may increase memory usage as new copies are created for modifications. Modern frameworks like System.Collections.Immutable in C# mitigate some of these issues with structural sharing.

Concurrency and Parallelism

Imperative Programming:

Managing shared mutable state in concurrent scenarios can lead to race conditions and complexity.

Functional Programming:

Immutability makes FP inherently safer and easier to reason about in concurrent and parallel systems.

Maintainability Comparisons

Code Readability

Imperative Programming:

Procedural code can become verbose and harder to follow as complexity grows.
Side effects and mutable state increase cognitive load for understanding the flow.

Functional Programming:

Declarative style emphasizes "what" is being done, making the code more concise and easier to read.

Example:
```csharp
Copy code
// Imperative
var evens = new List<int>();
foreach (var num in numbers)
{
    if (num % 2 == 0) evens.Add(num);
}
```

// Functional

var evens = numbers.Where(num => num % 2 == 0).ToList();

Testability

Imperative Programming:

Side effects and dependencies on shared state complicate testing.
Requires extensive mocking and setup for isolated tests.
Functional Programming:
Pure functions and immutability result in predictable outputs, simplifying testing.
No reliance on external state makes functions easier to test in isolation.

Scalability

Imperative Programming:

Can become unwieldy with increased functionality due to tightly coupled code and mutable state.
Functional Programming:

Encourages modularity and function composition, allowing easier scaling.

Example: Pipelines in FP can simplify processing large datasets.

Debugging and Error Handling

Imperative Programming:

Mutable state and side effects make it harder to track bugs.
Functional Programming:
Immutable state ensures fewer unintended changes, reducing debugging time.
Explicit error-handling patterns like the Maybe or Result types improve robustness.

When to Choose Each Paradigm

Functional Programming:

Best for applications requiring high reliability, concurrent processing, and maintainability, such as:

Financial systems

Real-time data pipelines
Reactive applications

Imperative Programming:

Suitable for performance-critical tasks and scenarios where mutability is essential, such as:

Game development
System-level programming

Hybrid Approaches in C#

C# allows developers to combine the strengths of both paradigms:

Use functional techniques (e.g., LINQ, immutability) for business logic.
Apply imperative constructs for performance-critical sections.

Example:
csharp
Copy code

```
var results = data.Where(x => x.IsValid).Select(x =>
Process(x)).ToList(); // FP
for (int i = 0; i < results.Count; i++) // IP
{
   Console.WriteLine(results[i]);
}
```

Conclusion

Functional programming excels in maintainability, testability, and safety, particularly in complex or concurrent systems. However, imperative programming remains advantageous in scenarios requiring raw performance or mutable state. C#'s versatility allows developers to blend these paradigms, leveraging the benefits of both for optimal results.

www.ingramcontent.com/pod-product-compliance
Lightning Source LLC
LaVergne TN
LVHW051437050326
832903LV00030BD/3137